THE BELLS
OF
TRURO

First published 1994

by

LANDFALL PUBLICATIONS
Landfall, Penpol, Devoran, Truro, Cornwall TR3 6NW
Telephone: 0872-862581

A CIP catalogue record for this book is available from
the British Library.

ISBN 1 873443 18 8

Typesetting by Bob Acton

Printed by the Troutbeck Press
and bound by
R. Booth Ltd., Antron Hill, Mabe, Penryn, Cornwall

Phyllis M. Jones

THE BELLS
OF
TRURO

Landfall Publications

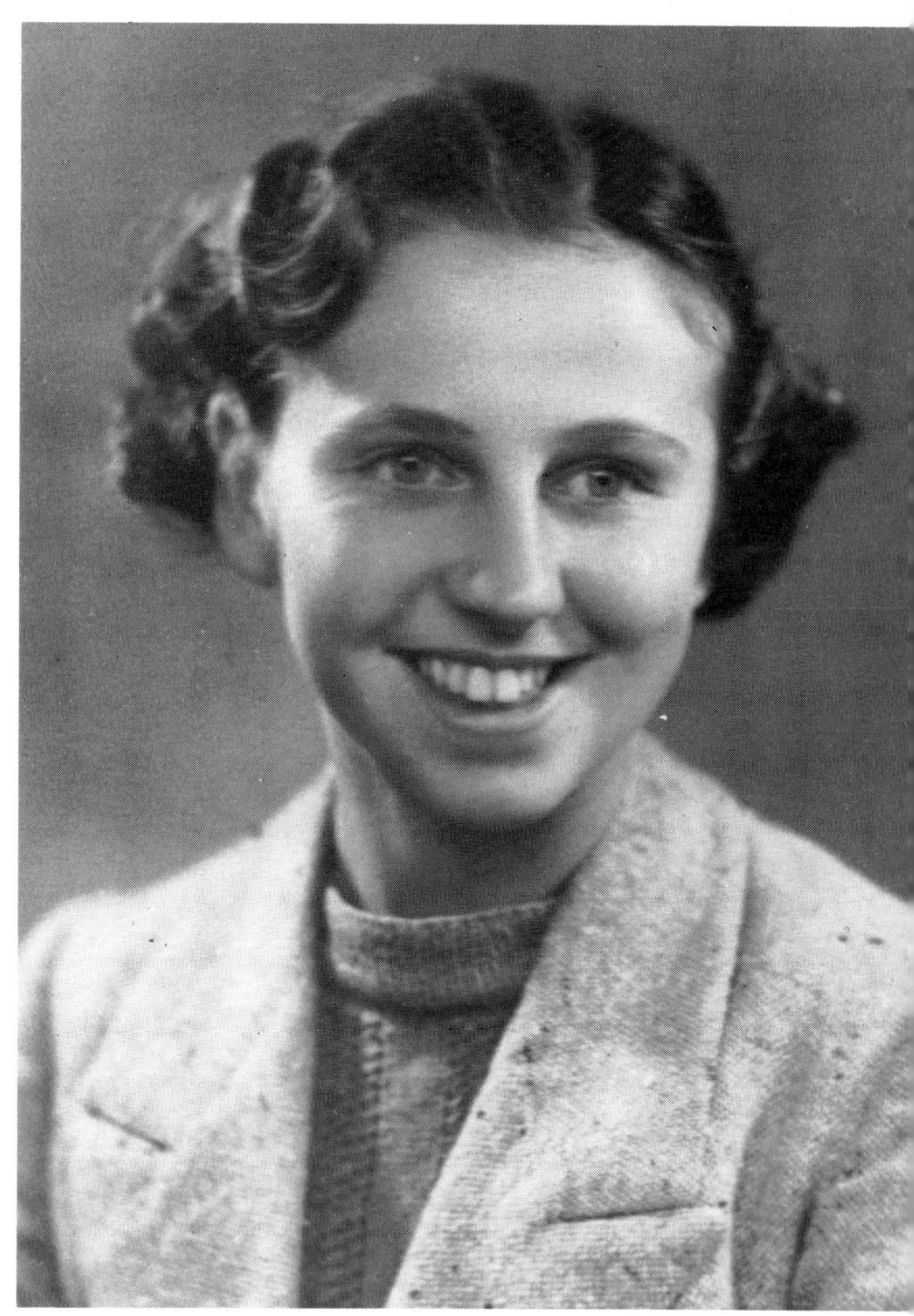

The author in her late teens

PHYLLIS MARJORY JONES (née Rule)

was born in Truro in 1923, the daughter of a Truro accountant, William James Rule, and his wife Mabel. She was educated at Truro County School for Girls, and it was during her last school holiday that the declaration of war in 1939 was heard over the radio.

After a brief interim period spent working in the Truro branch of Lloyds Bank, Marjory - as she was always called during her early years, and as she is still known in Cornwall - began training as a nurse in the Royal Cornwall Infirmary. Although she continued her work as a nurse (in different spheres) until she retired, she never relinquished her intense desire to write. *The Bells of Truro* shows that she was blessed in her young years: Cornwall was the background, between the English Channel and the Atlantic Ocean; there was a close and happy family, plenty of interesting aunts and uncles and lively cousins as well as her own brother and sister.

In retrospect young life might always appear idyllic, but the act of recording the memories never resulted in disappointment: it provided a new insight and a feeling that she and her contemporaries lived in an age of innocence.

At the end of her training, this time linked with the end of hostilities, Phyllis Marjory left her beloved Cornwall and was never to return except for holidays. She married Surgeon Lieutenant Cecil Vernon Arthur who was killed in 1959, and after a second happy marriage to Ivor Gordon Jones is now widowed (recently) for the second time.

Living in Wales she has put down new strong roots ... The Celtic bond *is* strong. As a writer, perhaps she is better known in that country, although she did win the Cornish Gorsedd Rose Bowl for poetry in 1970 and wrote for the *Cornish Review* and *Cornish Nation*. Her poetry and short stories have appeared in many established magazines, and her novel *There's Always the Park* was runner-up in an international competition for a novel of literary merit (run by the Society of Women Writers and Journalists). She has published four slim volumes of poetry: *Sailboats and Mackerel*, *Sylen*, *The Grass Has Not Yet Grown* and *Song of Gower*; and her book *They Gave Me a Lamp*, based on her experiences as a Colliery Nursing Officer at Cynheidre Colliery N.C.B., was widely acclaimed. She is a member of The Society of Authors, the Society of Women Writers and Journalists and the South West Writers Association. For many years she edited the quarterly publication for the Council for Protection of Rural Wales.

Her blue Cornish background is now replaced by the greener fields and mountains of Wales. She lives on a smallholding there, breeding beautiful Welsh Cobs and always writing.

From **Sailboats and Mackerel**

I am the child who scrabbles
Over boats at low tide
Like a sandfly;
I call through a maze of anchors;
My brown legs, spindling out of jeans,
Leap in the drumming madness
Of a primal Floral Dance.

The rounded sea walls are warmed
By sun; still they thrust
Wide shoulders against sea spray.
These stones are mine
And all the years when I trapped dreams.

CHAPTER ONE

Becoming a Part of Life

On the stony beach at Malpas, amongst the overturned boats, the deaf mute woman shrieked and waved her arms, the rags of her coat sleeves flapping in a grotesque emphasis.

At that time, for a shilling, it was possible to hire a boat, and our party was crossing over to Tolverne, a spot which was across the River Fal and a little further down, which I discovered in later years was to be a favourite. Why I remember this picnic with such clarity is hard to explain. Tolverne then was no more than a clearing in the wood, with a whitewashed cottage or two. In front of the window sills was a patch of grass, where the trestle table was laid with crockery and food, splits and cream, pasties and saffron cake. This was above the small, shaly beach, the edge of which was dark with long brown bootlace seaweed. Behind us, the woods were black-green. Chickens ran under the table and two dish-faced white Nanny goats wandered around us. My father's sister was there, Aunt Hilda and Mother and a vaguely visualised group of grown ups. It was a sultry day, and we had run down to the shore and back, over to the clearing, chased hens and teased the goats until we were tired. Who was there on that day beside my Mother and my Aunt? Who comforted me when I ran past the wild woman to reach the safety of Malpas Road on our return? Who held a coat over me when the summer sky was split with lightning and rain poured over us? Why did the picnic with the goaty faces and squawking chickens become such a separate and vivid incident in my childhood?

****** ****** ****** ****** ******

Myself as a round child in a check dress fixed in a wooden high chair ... and I recall the scraps of crumbs on the bleached tray in front of me. The dress was blue and in the little cobbled yard were galvanised buckets with floor-cloths drying and a worn-by-work-hands piece of smooth yellow soap. I can see the short bristles on the scrubbing brushes. Afterwards, as I heard so often, Old Man Whitford said to my Mother, 'You'll never rear

7

TOLVERNE ON THE R. FAL

that child, Mabel ... she's too good to live.' Words which were belied in the years to come. But in my mind I can see the next door neighbours, Emma Scantlebury and her daughter Winnie, and short, hare-lipped George, son and brother, whom somehow I connect with ladders. Shouts and quarrels and gossip and exchange of vital everyday information, like Emma's invitation to my Mother, 'Come in here, Mabel, Winnie's washing. Now look at her breasts. Feel the weight of 'em, Mabel.' Hearsay, but true. Like Emma's own saying, "Tis true, 'tis true ... 'tis true as I'm 'ere, 'tis true.' Next door to this family lived Auntie and my own Grandfather. Mother moved from our back door to their back door with cleaning brushes or covered plates, plates, sometimes steaming and sometimes carried carefully, as if there was a sumptuous treat which must not be spoilt ... probably it was no more special than a wobbling jelly. This was the time when my mother cared for the person who had sacrificed her life to look after four motherless girls, two sets of twins, at the request of her brother and my grandfather.

My grandmother, Mother's mother, died when she and her twin sister were eighteen months old. They were a second pair of twin girls. 'She was very beautiful,' my mother tells me, but as no one ever answered the young daughters' questions about her, that was about all they knew. Later the girls heard that she was feckless and drank. Well, gin was cheap and there was laughter to be had at the Duke of York, one of the roughest public houses in Truro. However, everyone who knew the family at the time said that Grandfather loved his wife to distraction, and when she died he was lost and devastated. He turned in his grief and bewilderment to his only sister and she answered his plea.

His sister Joan I can remember, albeit with some vagueness. She had iron-grey hair which she wore in a straight bob; a slide held it in place, dragging it away from her face, which was resigned and gentle and lined with suffering. She looked tired most times and her complexion was sallow. She must have missed out on the family's natural vitality, or perhaps this same vitality drained her of life. She was tall and thin and later she died of cancer. My own mother loved her, I think, as much as she ever truly loved anyone, and for ever appreciated the way Aunty, as everyone called her, had sacrificed so much to look after four motherless children.

There are good women and there are saints. Max Beerbohm wrote, 'Ordinary saints grow faint to posterity, while quite ordinary sinners pass vividly down the ages.' Aunty's sacrifice is difficult for an ordinary person to understand. Her desolate brother went up to Plymouth when grandmother died of pneumonia. He begged his sister to come home to keep house for him and to look after his children. Joan at this time was an

9

intelligent, attractive woman who was engaged as a companion to Frances Havergail, the hymn writer. She was about to be married and should have had her own family and home, but she put all this aside and returned to the cathedral city of Truro to look after her brother and the strange creatures who were his children. Mother says her first task was to make clothes for the children and she set about this by cutting up her own. She had little financial aid from her brother because he mistrusted all women's ability to handle money after his experience with his own wife. Besides, he would rather spend it on beer. Poor Aunty, for this is the name by which she was known from then onwards, had to take in sewing in order to have enough money for the children. Grandfer did supply the shoe leather.

****** ****** ****** ****** ******

Widening Rings

There were beginnings and there were stories of beginnings. If these could be separated, listed and filed, perhaps I might know which parts of me belonged to which of my forebears. As it is, I must grasp at fibres of memory and listen to voices which at times will murmur in the favourite places.

To record my brother's opinion, 'I was a queer child.' By this he meant I was lost in my own world, unable to express or perhaps not able to realise the potent childhood dreams, and therefore often in my frustration I chose to run away and trudged along brown, twining roads to strange places with determination to get somewhere, confident that before daylight faded someone would find me, take hold of a hand given with perfect trust, and lead me back into the heart of the family. In later years, an elderly lady with subtle understanding called me after Barrie's character, Mary Rose, the girl who was lost on an island. I was found quite easily because, always, my destination would be the little village of Calenick. In retrospect this was a collection of whitewashed cottages with a rounded wall on the bridge, where the locals gathered, as locals always will gather where there is the sound of water and a chance of scrutinising the passers by. The clock-tower and smelting house in the background mark that this backwater was once a scene of rural industry where there was a candle-making factory and a rope works and where an ancient corn mill was powered by the Nansavalon stream.

The cottages were low with small windows, roses trailing on thick, sturdy walls and thatched roofs, so in keeping against the wide hedgerows and, even now, I can feel the warmth which emanated from the small road between the foliage.

CALENICK

There were fundamental differences between the branches of the family, yet we did have security, and close bonds did exist which kept us together. The boy cousins might have been brothers, and my sister and I spent most of our holidays with one or other of the aunts.

The real dichotomy of the families lay between father's side and my mother's side, but even here contact and friendship were maintained. Mother's sisters were very much part of our lives. With them were the picnics, the feasts, the excitement, shared always by one or the other. These aunts were voluble and they made real to us all kinds of family lore. Once I said to my father, 'Your family never had such exciting lives as Mum's family. I wish you had more stories to tell.' He answered, 'I haven't got such a darn good imagination as your Mother.'

This was indeed the crux of the matter.

Father's mother was a tall, straight lady with a wide frame of white hair. Her face in the photograph which was taken when, I suppose, she was around fifty, was intelligent, sharp and etched with thoughtful expression lines. Only the other day in a letter from a cousin of my father to his sister, Grandma was mentioned ... 'I can see her lovely face now ... opposite me and listening ... her eyes encouraging me.' Her face did seem interesting. I would like to have known her like that cousin, to have had conversations with her and perhaps to have had her understand the strange, watchful child who was part of her and was her grandchild. However, if I am honest and admit how timid I was at that age, I know how her presence would intimidate. Visits to her small house where the lino was slippery with polish were never visits we anticipated with much pleasure. Grandma sat on her prickly, green upholstered chair with ram-rod straight back. 'As stiff as buckram' my mother said, as we sat between Sunday School time and Chapel time listening to our elders. I cannot remember what was discussed. To look at her she should have had a large house with a garden where children ran and played out their childhood. She should have watched from a verandah, serene, or reigned from a formal sitting room making the most of her natural presence. She was meant for a life quite different from her actual destiny which led to her bringing nine children into the world, seven of whom were brought up to be good Christian citizens and the other two dying in infancy. It must have been hard to provide for them. There must have been turmoil at times in that small house, and this I cannot imagine.

Her husband, our grandpa, was a round man with a floppy moustache. In later years he worked in a small house at the corner of City Road and Calenick Street which was taken over as a workshop. This was always filled with shavings and had the smell of resin and wood, and there was the sound of creaking or hammering. Before that he had been a

12

carpenter in a mine, out Idless way. Father told us how he had to take his father's lunch to him every day. This was the traditional pasty, wrapped in a white cloth. Everyone had pasties for dinner then, big, real, steaming pasties, and not sandwiches. This did mean a long walk for a boy during his school breaks, for it was about three miles.

There must have been quite a discussion when my grandparents were married, for Father's mother came from a good family. Her brothers were all Methodist Ministers and two actually went as missionaries. We have a brass Buddha which Uncle Edward brought back from his travels. When Uncle Edward was home on a visit, it was a ritual that he, with Grandpa and Grandma, came up to Carlyn, our house on the top of Daniell Road, where we were living at the time. It was inevitable that the family guests would have Sunday tea. Sylvia, my sister, and I would be dressed in best dresses and afraid to move. How proud we were in those blue velvet dresses with their fragile lace collars! There are photographs which show us in a formal group taken as we posed in the garden at home. Grandma in a chair, Uncle Edward and Grandpa behind her, Mother and my brother Howard, whose white, white collar contrasted with his dark Sunday suit and dark skin, ranged on either side of them, Sylvia and I curled at their feet. The tea itself would be as disastrous as our meals always were when Mother tried hard to emulate her mother-in-law. The saffron cake would be dry and, in spite of jelly having been made on the previous evening, the meal would be late.

Sunday comes. We play a prim charade, dried peas and dark meat and Church, and there is the soaring thought and walks through Sunday lanes. Drinking tea in afternoon quiet, always at four; awaiting release in rustling light, in shadows when musk emanates, infiltrating dusk.

Why were my mother's family not considered respectable? Was it because they lived on the other side of the tracks, social distinctions just as marked in the poorer part of the town? Did they have a few more skeletons in the cupboard or was it their vitality which made certain any such skeletons would dance with more abandon? Yet my maternal grandfather was a carpenter also, and what is more he was a cabinet maker and had worked on the carving in Truro Cathedral. How important was that work which changed the whole character of Truro, when St Mary's Church, ancient and impressive, was incorporated into the fabric of the Cathedral! If I look at the seats of other woodwork in the building, I wonder, did he, my own grandfather carve this? Their family name was Wilnor. I like to think this bears out the legend that his father was washed up on the beach at Portscatho after a shipwreck during a severe storm. Will from the sea, in the old Cornish language, very much distorted. Old Mother Pascoe told this story because she says she remembers it and she was over a hundred years old when she died. We do know that my grandfather would have told us anything. I have one photograph of 'Grandfer' taken when he visited us while we were on holiday at Porthtowan. He was dressed in the contemporary heavy suit with collar and tie, and having walked from the bus stop over a sandy road in summer heat, he stopped to rest on a boulder. He was mopping his forehead with a red spotted handkerchief. If the camera could have recorded all his cursing and swearing for posterity, well, there would have been a true memorial.

In fairness I must admit that I have seen the wedding certificate of Grandfather and he had the same name as his father, Charles Olver Wilnor, who was put down on the certificate as a sailor but did not sign. 'Olver' is a family name which was given to my brother and has always caused speculation because it is a surname and not a Christian name. My mother said that at the contemporary census there were no other Wilnors. They were married at St Michael's Church, Baldhu. My Grandfather's mother, whose name was Cordelia, died on December 11th 1877.

****** ****** ****** ****** ******

Truro, when viewed from the surroundings, is dominated by the Cathedral with its three spires and one Church tower which is green. The Church Tower is made of copper and has enough verdigris on it to kill all the population, they say. Our lives seemed to be always within the sound of cathedral bells, when we lived in the streets of the town itself and later when we moved to the top of the hill, Daniell Road, my father having some success in his career as an accountant. Always we heard the sound of the cathedral bells and the chimes of the town clock. Later the bells became especially evocative and reminded us of those Sundays spent with Aunt Delia in her small house in the street of St Clement.

When my mother was young she lived in Tabernacle Street which was in the poorer part of town. It led to Lemon Quay and the Green. She remembers this street with ocean-going ships, barges and sailboats and I think I do too. The fair was held on the Green each Whitsun and at the bottom of Tabernacle Street, as on any other wharves, were all the buildings which are found when business is connected with foreign trade and ships. In the small, narrow street there was the blacksmith, also places where lime could be bought for a penny per bucket and herrings were 'six a penny'. There was a station on one side of the river, at Newham, opposite Malpas Road, and when the circus came to town all the caged animals were placed in the sidings and then loaded on to the trailers with steam rollers and the travelling people with their animals paraded through the town, the children following with shouts and laughter. Mother tells us she once saw a dancing bear.

My maternal grandmother belonged to the Webbers who brought energy and force into the stock: tin miners, seamen and lovely dark-eyed women who stood up to the stress in those tough days. They came from Threemilestone, Hugus, Kea and Baldhu. Their names are engraved on the headstones in Kea Churchyard. All these places are threaded with small roads. I wonder, is it the spirit of our ancestors who created an atmosphere in those lanes which drew us mysteriously when we were children? The gas works were near, and as children we were fascinated by the rising and falling of those huge cylinders. One day there was an explosion, and we ran into the streets as did everyone else in the area. One of the containers blew up. I can remember the frightening noise and the sounds from the crowd of people who gathered so suddenly in Fairmantle Street. Strangely I can recall the exact spot. We were standing on the pavement outside Fairmantle Street School.

****** ****** ****** ****** ******

Truro is between the Atlantic and the English Channel. It was sited at the head of the Truro River but long since the water has been pushed back by the flow of silt from the many small rivers which have run down from the hills and there is now a car park where once the masts of ships were seen at Lemon Quay. The River Fal is wide, a tidal river with green woods on either side, and it spreads into glossy, shadowed creeks as it reaches Falmouth Harbour. From the town the river went past warehouses which smelt of malt and where we walked warily because of rats, and then there was the silty mud where all logs were laid to season before being made into quality furniture. These were a dangerous playground for us. We leaped over them or bounced as they rocked in the slithering mud and ran foolhardy races from one end of the pile to the other. Later the river passed two parks and reached the stony beach at Malpas which had a ferry to St Michael Penkevil. To be ferried across we had to give a piercing whistle to alert the ferry man and his bent figure would be watched as he came from his cottage and untied the boat on the opposite shore. We did not appreciate that this was the route followed by Tristan and Isolde during their tragic love affair.

Narrow streets through old buildings were the pathways we knew well, each one the haunt of a memory. There was a longer walk which I remember, an organised walk by the Brown Owl, to Kenwyn and beyond. I sat in the corner of our kitchen, in Father's chair, and watched as Mother bustled between table and stove. I was waiting for the saffron buns to come out of the oven. At last the tray of yellow, yeasty-smelling buns was ready, laid out on the table before being placed on the baking tray. I did what we always did, and that was to pick one up, throw it between my hands until it was cool enough to handle and be ready for that first bite into the soft baked dough. Time passed swiftly; I jammed on my Brownie cap and ran down the hill, across the town to High Cross, the square outside the Cathedral where we were supposed to meet. There was no other Brownie in sight. Someone must have pointed me in the right direction because I followed their trail but never caught up with the party, in fact I did not even catch a glimpse of them. I was young and frightened when I entered into Kenwyn Churchyard; I suppose there must have been something familiar about the little gate and the way past different gravestones. I must have known. Probably the grave on which I sat was one I had seen before, but for ever after it was a miracle which was quoted over and over again. I was sitting on Auntie's grave when Mother's sister, Aunt Delia, just happened to visit the grave on that particular Saturday to put her bunch of flowers in the glass jam-jar. She stared at me. 'Marjory,' she half whispered, her own face looking scared. I answered her. It was just another time when someone would arrive to take me home when I was lost after one of my excursions. How proudly she tip-tippled up to our house on her high-heeled black patent shoes (her one concession to fashion) when she returned her tear-stained niece.

Discovery of ways out of my home town was, in retrospect, a series of walks through mouldering hedgerows with brown, muddy patches which, after our constant use, made steps to the top of the hedge from which point we saw damp fields in winter or luxuriant green fields in summer rising towards the next horizon. The horizon was softened with trees when we looked.towards the South and Falmouth but cleared into sky and space towards the North and the Atlantic.

Some incidents are unforgettable. The blood staining the waters of a pool and spreading red into a small stream which was the scene of carnage when a neighbour's dog which was in our care killed two young geese. There was the hunter's yelp and the beating of wings and honk honking of the geese, white wings which were marked with blood. My sister and I took the dog and ran from our first taste of violence. We were quiet when we returned and could not find words to tell our parents what had happened. It could not have been too difficult for the farmer to discover just who had walked towards that little stream because our secret was soon to be brought into the open. The farmer rang the bell to face my father. He asked Dad if he had two small daughters who had a dog. That day I remember the first steely words from my father and learnt, with certainty, that it pays to be honest and to own up, whatever the crime.

KENWYN CHURCHYARD

Penwhithers Lane was our own walk. ("Penwhithers" is the spelling I knew as a child; maps and signs show it as "Penwethers" or "Penweathers" nowadays.) It might be a gentle exercise around the block but it was a road which led to the open moorland and to Wheal Jane which was then an old tin mine but which was later to be restarted to rejuvenate the industrial scene in Truro. A little further to the softer side, to the South, there was a farm which belonged to the Thomas family, Aunt Delia's husband's brother. In the beginning it was a place where they grew violets and anemones for the flower market. Willy and his wife Annie both had hard, bony faces which seemed as if they had been stripped of flesh by the hardness of their work.

One visit which I must describe happened on a day, just after Christmas, when most of the larders were well stocked and when we walked to the farm in response to an invitation. Aunt Annie was proud of her son Elwyn but Elwyn was nowhere to be seen; he had hidden himself somewhere in the rooms above the kitchen.

His mother called, 'Come down my little bird.' She cried over and over, 'Come down and meet your cousins from Truro.'

Elwyn did not answer and only rustles told us he was still up there.

She called many times and at last a large, lumbering boy in his best short trousers came down to disillusion us. He glared and chewed his way through tea and supper as all of us from the sophisticated streets of Truro regarded him with a touch of superiority.

Perhaps I remember most vividly the long walk home when the bright cold moon threw bare oaks and alder trees into black shapes and there was a frosty taste of air, and how, with much chattering and singing and cuddling up to our parents, we returned home. It was a slow walk because 'Granfer' was with us and he slowed the pace. We did not mind for after our supper of ham and mince pies, jelly and splits and, almost definitely, saffron cake, we were content.

Destiny always surprises. The little lout that we met that day was later to become a very successful auctioneer in Truro and was to hold court in the Market on Wednesdays for many years. The gauche and silent boy had discovered the gift of the gab and, it was said, he could sell anything.

Another road led up the steep Campfield Hill and out into the country. I wondered often about the name for this mysterious hill and its purpose, yet never thought details like this might ever be significant. Looking at an old engraving one sees this area is marked and it must have been where armies set out their camps ... Moresk , Newham and Malpas, little old places have been the settings for love stories, battles, myths and legends, and I took them all for granted, only feeling the bond which grew stronger with the years.

Becoming a Part of Life

Truro was a thriving town
When Falmouth was a furzy down.

We walked up Campfield Hill once when we went to a sale in a country house to buy a dining room table which had been advertised. It was a long, summer walk which was a typical Cornish walk through steep hedges, so thick with grass that we could fling ourselves into the green as if was a cushion.

If ever I think of Summer I shall remember the narrow heat of the road between full, past-their-best, blowing grasses. How the thrust of young ash trees supported brambles, and how sweet-smelling and warm were the white heads of cow parsley which towered for position. Sometimes a patch of short grass altered the texture of the hedgerow and white or pink clover coloured a small area of green. Sometimes the heavy sweetness which pervaded the long winding road was enhanced by more exotic perfumes from honeysuckle or wild rose.

Summer echoed with humming, winged insects, the sound of which, once caught, expanded, like a low note in an orchestra, right through the hot air and the bushes, brambles and trees, above the thin trickle of a stream, and there was the tired twittering of hidden birds, so that the whole afternoon was filled with a buzzing drone.

And the house, pushed against oaks and beech trees, looked as if expectant of a new owner, almost as if it might be glad. Geraniums filled the windows and brought even more plant-life into the heart of the home.

From this spot came the dining table of dark oak with thick carved legs which was destined for the new house at the top of Daniell Road.

The Leats with the Chainfields are parts of a way out of Truro which is associated with vivid fragments of my childhood forming tangible memories. Even now I can feel the summer glare of that squalid street, the dust and hot pavements, harsh shadows; the heat which was part of my first awareness. A sound of a bell would send us running from chalky classrooms to the back streets which we favoured and which led to the civic park with its wrought-iron bandstand. Here we would run over burnt, brown grass, following paths through flower beds, chasing each other, watching the High School pupils play their organised tennis as they raised clouds of dust with every point they made.

Most times we passed Old Mother Morris's house, older and smaller than its neighbours. A house which was different because of the slow-moving trough of water between the garden wall and the pathway.

This sombre water, almost dormant, was filled with black water-creatures, green slime, old tin cans and other rubbish. In Summer, mosquitoes hovered over its evil depths. The water found an escape through a grating and a way along an old subterranean passage which led under the town to the river. There were water rats where the water reappeared, hundreds of them, as in the pictures of 'The Pied Piper of Hamelin.'

This stretch of water never failed to fascinate us. There was an old drainpipe leading across it and we took turns to walk this. Always we had to be driven by a dare and no one ever refused. The water was not deep but we had heard so many stories of drunks drowning in the green slime that it had an thrilling aura which drew us to its edge.

'The Leats', and my heart pumps like an engine in my chest. There was the old lady's cottage with the paint on her doors faded and peeling; the curtains, yellow with grime and in shreds; there were cats, everywhere ... tabbies, persians, ginger toms and black and whites; all of them with dusty coats and hungry faces; green eyes, demanding and fierce eyes.

We lingered as a ritual at this particular spot, lured by the water, the old cottage, the cats and most of all by 'Old Mother Morris'. We had a heathenish game of calling up the old woman.

'Come on, it's your turn.'

It always seemed to be my turn.

'No... I'll walk the plank instead.'

'You did that yesterday. Go on. I'll dare you.'

'I'll dare you.'

'I cried first.'

Whoever was chosen would cross the pipe, go through the open gateway and knock loudly on her front door. Then we would turn and retreat with mad haste back to the footpath. Once safe amongst the gang we would wait for the old lady to appear. She would come to the door and peer down the path. She would rave in her cracked voice. 'Be off, you varmints. Can't you leave an old body alone? Shame on you, you dirty rascals. Be off or I'll have the skin off your backs.'

'Old Mother Morris, tell us a story!' we would chant over and over again.

'A story? Where's my stick. I'll give you tales!' she would come to the gate and yell at us across the Leats.

We knew, even if she attempted it, that we could be out of her range by the time she crossed. We continued ... 'Come on ... just one.'

She would stand by the old tree by the gate and look at us. Sometimes she would shrug and go back in. Sometimes she would say, 'What do you want to hear about?'

We'd say ... 'The old tin mines when you used to be a Bal Maiden, or tell us about the river and the rats and the old rat woman.'

She would begin by saying ... ' You children don't know nothing about it. You've had it easy ... all of you. I remember what it was to be real hungry.' Sometimes she'd ramble.

'I never knew till later on. When I was young it was always the others who were starving. They were rough, they'd shout at us in the streets.'

For a moment she'd stop and look at us, wondering perhaps why people shouted if one was rich or if one was poor.

'I knew a man once who stole fourpence to buy bread and was sent to prison ... but that's nothing you'd care about. What d'you want to know?'

We would wait.

'I'll tell you about the boy who thought he could say where the tin veins ran or where there was copper ... just by standing alone on the headlands. He'd point with his hand and there they would sink a shaft. And sure enough he'd be right.'

Once she began telling her story her voice lost the rough Cornish accent and became refined and gentle. To us she sounded alien. Our parents said she was an educated woman who had come down in the world.

Once when one of her cats had been chased up to the top of the tree by a dog, I climbed up to get it down for her. The cat clawed my shoulders and scratched my arms and I slid back to the ground against the sharp bark of the tree. The wild, ungrateful animal drew still more blood as she leapt from my shoulder to her mistress.

Old Mother Morris insisted that I came inside her house so that she could bathe my cuts. I was without fear, almost, when I entered her cottage because I wanted to explore the dark mystery of her home. What a scoop! I could see envy on each one of my friends' faces.

She led me to a tiny room filled with old heavy furniture. The springs of the armchairs showed through the horse-hair in places. It was shadowed, but a fire smouldered in the grate, and a kettle was boiling, held close to the fire by a round piece of iron on a swivel. She had an old piece of linen, which, in contrast to everything else, was clean and white. She poured something in the water and the steamy, pungent mixture was poured over my wounds. She talked and talked. Now I forget everything except the words which stuck in my mind ... ' Knowledge is power.' When she said this the conviction in her voice conveyed a ringing truth to the phrase.

Perhaps she is a witch, I thought, confirming our long-held opinions, but somewhere inside of me there was a, then unrecognised, affinity with her, which later I began to understand.

Becoming a Part of Life

****** ****** ****** ****** ******

In this mysterious interlude of childhood, inside the first rings after the pebble had dropped into life's pool there must be the sound of the Floral Dance.

Distant recollections of the long walk taken by all the town children out of the centre of the city to the top of Daniell Road, along Treyew Road to the Green, our Green, the field in Treyew Road which overlooked the town. We walked or hopped in pairs to the sound of music, pagan music, and even now, if I should catch a phrase of that music from any modern source I throb with the old emotion. In ancient days they went to bring in the May in connection with who knows what Celtic sacrificial rites. 'I'm to be Queen of the May, Mother, I'm to be Queen of the May.' Feared giants made of wattle which darkened blood memories, and the saffron bun, spiced before sacrifice. To us children the large saffron bun was nicer than any we had at home. It was a brighter yellow and had much more fruit in it. We ran and played all afternoon and then gathered for the main Floral Dance back into Truro ... dancing every step of the way with older people who could not contain themselves as soon as they heard the primal beat of the band ... all the time more people joined hands and the crowd became larger and larger.

CHAPTER TWO

Sound of Cathedral Bells

Eddying rings mark wider family memories which are bound to involve our maternal aunts. Their vibrant selves transformed their homes, ordinary houses, into places of entertainment, mystery, fun and the pathos and courage which we never appreciated until later in our lives.

A landmark so definite in retrospect was when, as a family, we were taken in by Aunt Delia for thirteen weeks when Mother became ill. These must have been thirteen long weeks for her to endure, our kind, sometimes suppressed and always put-upon Aunt Delia. Even in the days of the extended family, it was an unselfish act to take a family of five into her small, two-up-and-two-down cottage when she had to care for her own, rather demanding husband and son.

We were small and when I look back the whole time is blurred and hazy, but details do stand out with clarity. There was the ride across town with our baggage stacked outside the black-leathered 'cab' while we swayed gently inside to the rhythm of the horses' trot.

We soon were welcomed into the home of our uncle and aunt and must have overflowed the space in every room. In Aunt Delia's kitchen the grained table and the Cornish Range had pride of place. There were two oak arm-chairs on either side of the grate and here we spent our time. I retain one memory which was the sinister spectre of Uncle Robert's cork leg which rested at the side of the bed and could be seen quite clearly from the landing on top of the stairs if we passed when he was resting. It seemed to have a life of its own, one leg standing with half a pair of trousers on it. During the daytime my uncle controlled his disability very well, in fact it seemed to give him an unfair advantage. He hopped around with dexterity. His walking stick was his sword, and the boys, Raymond, his son and my brother, Howard, kept well out of the sweeping circle which protected him and attacked those who offended.

St Clement Street was one of the many small streets which made up the old Truro along with others, like St Austell Street, Old Bridge Street, St Mary's Street and the previously mentioned Campfield Hill. Even in those days, they had lost some of their previous importance which their names

ST CLEMENT ST

proclaim, and were the back lanes from the Cloisters and the town itself. Old Bridge Street passed the rear of the Red Lion. As children we made this our meeting place where we gathered and sniffed the smell of dung or oil for hooves and harness. We watched the coachmen grooming the horses. Large shining horses they were ... Trixie, Joanna, Tommy, Prince, they were used in those pre-taxi days as transport for those who were not quite rich enough to have their own horse and carriage; the grooms were close still to the traditions of the previous travellers. But it was next door to No. 16 St Clement Street that the Post Coach and horse was kept after it had collected the mail from Truro Station each working morning. Under an arch separating the road from his yard, the horses clopped over cobbles to the stables and shelter owned by Mr. Tapp. His horses, Trooper, Billy, Mick, Tom and Charlie, we knew more intimately. Trooper was a war hero: he had taken his part in World War 1.

Inside the walls of this little house we heard with almost Quasimodo proximity the sound of Cathedral bells. It was here that Uncle grabbed each boy on Sunday mornings and, under the iron pump which stands, even at this moment, in the yard, scrubbed them without mercy. With rough ceremony Howard and Raymond were cleaned of the week's grime, receiving so often a blow that it later became known as the Sunday clout. Sylvia and I, much more comfortably, were washed by Aunt Delia as we were seated on the kitchen table.

Now I am able to appreciate the sacrifices which were made by her, Aunt Delia who was so beautiful that an artist staying near Truro asked permission once to paint her. She retained this beauty and had her special look ... dark hair, grey eyes, large and sparkling, an oval face with dimples and a pale creamy complexion. Her expression was endowed by nature but it was a cruel fact that her selflessness was never seen in its true perspective, not by us wilful children, nor her sisters and never by her husband. When we were older, if any one of us made a gesture entailing some self-denial, it was known in the family as 'doing an Aunt Delia.' In spite of her 'paddling along' as she called it, and everything that was soft and gentle and sometimes fearful when clashing with her domineering husband, the thing that stopped her being a push-over was her devastating wit. The cutting down to size - after all, she was a tailoress, with an apt phrase, not ever intended to hurt but able always to deflate. Anyone who was too big for his boots was fair game. 'What you know will fill a book, what you don't know will fill a library.' 'If you fell into the sea you'd come up with a diamond necklace.' 'Take off that hat, Mabel, it's making a draught.' Other more original and earthy comments were made which were laced with a bit of her own back-street language. Her complexion was white, not as if she were ill nor colourless: it was translucent almost, not needing colour to give it life. Before making one of her devastating comments, her lips would compress, the corners of her mouth would tremble, her grey eyes would turn towards us and we could see the glint of humour before the muttering began. 'One thing Mabel, you'll never wear yourself out.' When she was out of range, 'I don't know how you ever caught me, Robert ... with your cork leg.'

If we think of Christmas we are bound to think of Aunt Delia. Her Christmas spreads included everything that Dickens could have recalled in his own Christmas scenes. Goose for Christmas lunch which as a family we shared was traditional at No. 16. We arrived on Christmas mornings to sit by her roaring fires in our feathery, new Christmas slippers. Tradition meant we spent Christmas Day with Aunt Delia and Uncle Robert and all other members of mother's family and on Boxing Day my Mother and Father were the hosts. Our lunch consisted of a turkey with the Christmas pudding. Tradition meant that Mother was late, always. As a guest she would arrive smiling and panting at the last moment, just in time to sit down; as a hostess she smiled from her corner in our kitchen as her sisters puffed in the steam created from cooking Mother's own feast. Christmas in those Truro years remained the same even when Aunt Delia and family moved from St Clement Street to Fairmantle Street.

I recall the times after those ham and pickled onion suppers ended when it was almost midnight and there was a prospect of a long walk back to Carlyn, up St Aubyn's Road, through a back lane and along Strangways Terrace, past the house where a mad woman came out on moonlit nights, carrying a candle, and talked to a goat and a donkey in an opposite field. If this prospect daunted overmuch, we stayed for the night. The feather bed with its hollows warmed by a stone hot-water bottle was cosy. Aunt Delia would say, 'Now then, you maidens, say your prayers and go to sleep.' For a while we would watch Aunt Delia, cloaked in her roomy nightgown, fumble with corset hooks as she undressed with the same modesty she would have shown on a beach, if she ever undressed on a beach. We would not sleep until we made sure she came in the middle of us so that we could cuddle into her warm, flannely softness and hear her chuckling endearments.

What was essentially Aunt Delia's own, her one real obsession, was her passion for the Whitsun Fair. We saw but never knew why this should be, at least, not then. Yet, thinking back to Mother's account of their childhood, to the time when the riverside area of Newham, which was the end of the railway-line, and seemed to be so important to Aunt Delia, it was this which must have been the beginning. She would be one of the children racing down to the station to see the travellers arrive. Her own life was drab and her mind was exuberant ... she would see the vividly

THE BACKYARD AT ST CLEMENT ST

dressed women with their gipsy scarves, earrings and beads adorning them; dark-eyed men might tease her and there would be the bustle of arrival, hard work made lighter by laughter and comments in different dialects. Another world which, for a moment she could smell, reach towards and nearly touch. So what happens later? Once a year when the Fair comes to Truro Green the magic is renewed.

On the Green the painted lorries and waggons appeared on Mondays. For a while, hammering and banging, shouting and engine sounds prevailed and by evening there would be steam organ music. It was then that Aunt Delia's face came alive. Every night with a 'cheeld' led from each hand she walked with Sylvia and me to the Fair. Even as children we never got as much pleasure from the fairground as did our aunt. She would loiter outside the green and red rails of the Noah's Ark or Dodgems and watch until the last rides, getting shorter and shorter, would cease. With our Fairings, nougat, the odd celluloid doll and always fish and chips in our newspaper packet, we would return home.

The fair remained her delight up to and during the last years of her life.

When Mother broke her collar bone, there was a family crisis and this of course was the reason we moved, as a family, to the house in St Clement Street and inflicted ourselves on Aunt Delia. A broken collar bone does not seem to have been a serious thing, not enough to warrant those long weeks away from our own home. Mother, however, was seriously ill. In retrospect it seems as if she was suffering from a nervous breakdown and during this period she was to win her lasting victory over all those who loved her. She said to me when she was in her seventies that she had confided in me most of the family stories. I think she did. I suppose this might have been because I was interested. Later on I recorded many of them. The later versions were sometimes embellished, but they reminded me of tales I knew. How often I had sat opposite her on the kitchen table to listen as she dwelt on her past!

'Your Father said, when I was lying on my bed ... close to my end, what with my bad chest and being so run-down and having no heart to go on ... "Mabel," he said, "what should I do if you went? What of the children?" D'you know, from then on, I kind of got my strength from somewhere.'

She told me another time, 'I was so depressed. Depression is awful you know. The doctor said, "You've got to fight it." He looked up at the canary. He said - I could not make it out at the time - "Does that bird sing?" "A bit," I said. "Well, when it sings, you sing with it." ' She smiled as she remembered. 'Well, the bird began chirping the next day. I didn't feel like singing, but I did. The only song I could think of was "Tell me the old, old story, of Jesus and his love." I sang it over and over, until Billy, the bird, knew it as well as I did.'

Later I understood, her breakdown was caused by overwork. The last thing that her ungrateful children ever suspected of her. She had three young children then and a husband just starting up on his own as an Accountant after years of studying. The strain of keeping us quiet must have been a problem on its own. Besides this, two doors away, her rather selfish father lived with her frail aunt. She had two homes to look after in the days when housework was not lightened by the machines and gadgets we have.

She was, it seems, a bit highly strung and she suffered from frequent epileptic fits. It was during one of these she broke her collar bone. Her breakdown was severe.

Her twin sister, our Aunt Flo, was a more robust character. We knew whenever the two of them were together, Aunt Flo, the extravert, assumed, as her right, the role of the star, and Mother, instead of making the most of her own attributes - her business sense, her interest in learning, her skill in dress-making - did not develop her own style but tried, without success, to compete.

There was also the problem of trying to live up to my Father's own family ambitions for him. I was told that they did try to stop their marriage, not at the time, as if we would have cared that she was pregnant when they were married.

The pity of it all. The shame she must have felt, deep enough to last until their Golden Wedding, afraid to celebrate this in case the secret would escape.

So, when she was ill, she latched on to that moment of power when her Will pleaded with her to fight, not to die. She learnt the possibilities in making everyone else feel guilty.

CHAPTER THREE

Central House and Christopher Crab

We were lucky to have Aunt Flo in Falmouth and Aunt Gertie in St Mawes. These two places were on opposite sides of the River Fal. This was a wide sparkling river which flowed broadly into the English Channel. Two castles, round-turreted and grey on green banks marked the headlands of the respective sea towns. They were built in the time of King Henry VIII and both were in states of good repair. In St Mawes and Falmouth we absorbed the atmosphere and beauty of Cornwall and learned so much which was necessary for a balanced and happy childhood.

Central House was important in our lives. Each room had its different smell and character. Each room had an atmosphere. Perhaps it was the square kitchen, which remained a family room when the house was filled with Aunt Flo's paying guests. Maybe it was the piano room where Frank played Boogie-woogie on the piano, vamping over the keys and where we played charades or danced whenever there was a party in the New Year which was Aunt Flo's Christmas celebration and when she cooked her duck. Maybe it was the gramophone room where records sounding weak and reedy scratched away, sound coming from a kind of light oak box; the tune I recall being played mostly was Amy Johnson's song, 'Wonderful Amy'. This was the current favourite. Amy Johnson, famous for her solo flights, was touring the country at the time and Mother and Aunt Flo had to join the crowd at Falmouth Station to see her on the evening she was expected.

Amy Johnson stepped off the carriage on to the platform and found herself face to face with two smiling women who were holding two small girls between them. She greeted them with all dignity demanded by the occasion and did not realise that she was ignoring the official party. The Mayor, weighed down by his chain, and the reception committee, dressed in some of the best dresses from Falmouth shops, waited with formality behind the barriers, and that did not have the desired impact.

In the kitchen at Central House there was a black Cornish Range from which oven Felix the cat was rescued, barely in time, on one baking-day morning. Here, the kitchen table was always ready for meals, or for the preparation of same, or for the serious card-reading which all four sisters found interesting. At times, when nothing was going on except a dutiful wait for Uncle Charlie to come in for tea, for something to finish cooking in the oven or ... anything, Aunt Flo would entertain. She would walk with the presence of a Prima Donna to the centre of the floor, lift up the corner of her apron to wipe her eyes and then with a sobbing voice sing,

'Ring down the curtain, I cannot sing tonight
My heart is breaking, I cannot sing tonight...
Now then girls, don't laugh ... it's true ... My heart is breaking ...'

I can see her now as she stood sometimes, on the flagstones behind the stable door which was then the passage door. Brown eyes with a sharp, bright, smiling look which seemed to be asking all around to share a joke.

It was not always a joke. This time her words were accusing. 'Don't tell me you maids 'ave missed our Christopher again.'

I wanted to cry. Every day it was the same. Christopher Crab who lived in the rock pool by Jumper's Rock came to Central House especially to see us and now, once again we were too late. Yesterday we were too early.

'Maybe 'ee won't come down today being as you wouldn't see 'un yesterday. I'd run down to the beach, you know where 'ee lives. 'Ee was put out, mind.'

Sylvia and I caught hands and raced along the road to Castle Beach which was our own beach for years and years. We would be nice to Christopher, make friends and everything, that is, if we could see him.

At dinner time when we returned, Aunty Flo, in her faded apron, a washed-out blue or pink, would be getting out dinners for her 'guests' or for us. She would be calm and happy as she ladled out cabbage, carrots and roast potatoes in spite of the long working table which covered the bath in the back kitchen being a cluttered mess. It was one thing at a time for Aunty Flo; during the morning after she had rid herself of her energetic nieces, she was able to proceed with her cooking and housework unencumbered.

Then there were the afternoons.

Afternoons were spent on the beach with Aunt Flo and a group of her cronies; this was a mixture of her neighbours and some of the shopkeepers from the main, narrow street of Falmouth; Mrs. Maggs was one name I remember. No one else used Castle Beach in those days. The women brought bread, butter, cheese and anything which was handy in their kitchens. Always pasties and saffron cake were included, that being our staple diet. A kettle was boiled when the children had searched for, and brought back bleached sticks which added blue flames to the little fire being

31

built inside the ring of round beach pebbles. Tea lasted all afternoon. The women gossiped. Children played on the grey, gravelly sand or on the rocks or in the water. There was a mixture of sensations: sharp sand between our toes, squelchy bladder-wrack under our feet as we clambered over the rocks uncovered at low tide, burnt skin peeling from our shoulders, warm low pools in which we lay ... and Jumper's Rock, a combination of large and small rocks with an intervening gap over which we dared each other to jump. Years later I looked at that gap and wondered how we had the nerve even to try this dangerous feat.

After six o'clock the men began to arrive, their day's work having finished. Uncle Charlie, in a striped flannel shirt and grey trousers, was the only one who changed, his dark pin-striped undertaker's suit being too precious to be spoilt by sand and sea-water. Once more in retrospect I wonder at the thickness and the warmth of that flannel shirt on a summer's day. Then the sound of gossip changed its timbre, men's laughter merged with shriller screams from the women and, as we grew 'tired and teasy' as our grown-ups would say, tearful outbursts from the children.

When evenings were long no one thought of getting supper until nine o'clock at least. Supper, when it began, lasted until after dark and longer. We might see the moon stretch out towards the Manacles as we ate our fried fish or sausages or bacon and eggs and fried Hog's Pudding. Ash under the everboiling kettle piled white in the hollow between the stones. Not until midnight sometimes, or when the last word had been said and contented silence fell between the members of that old-time barbecue, was the beach furniture gathered under brown arms prior to the trail up the cliff path, past the white, impressive Falmouth Hotel, along Beach Road and home. We entered the warm interior of Central House, and piled into the beds which we probably filled with sand.

Remembered particularly in Falmouth were Easter Walks. On Easter Sundays we would walk around the Castle Drive with Dad. There was a view of the harbour and sea right the way round the whole of the road. We would stop at Melvill Gardens to run down through the lawns to the rocks; we would stop at Castle Point to look at St Mawes Castle and to go as far as we could out to the point which was the landmark for many a famous sailor including those who have sailed the Atlantic in small craft in more recent times. Above the docks we would linger. Howard, my brother, studied the comings and goings of these large ocean-going ships which were in for refit or repair all his life; the interest was born in these early years. Along the Drive there were seats at strategic places. As if it was essential to mark our presence in this corner of Falmouth we would be certain to sit on each one. We knew the feel of the wood grain, the number of carvings and exactly which plants grew around the bench.

CASTLE BEACH
FALMOUTH

In the evenings there would be a long walk across the front to Swanpool and around, past the graveyard where lay Uncle Charlie first, and many years later Aunty Flo, who stipulated, 'I'm not going to be burnt, I'm going to lie beside my Charlie.'

This walk was in the other direction, towards the west, when we walked along the tarmacadamed pavement, passing those other beaches along the sea front which were never our own.

The earliest walks in company with Father and Sylvia seem now a series of impressions, a broken line in the texture of the pavement where a little subsidence had taken place; the heat which bounced back on those summer days and which was felt through thin soles of our sandals; quick rushes away from the steady movement of Father down to the shore, sometimes to clamber over the line of rocks to rejoin him further along, or to have a quick peep through the lower entrance of Gyllyngdune gardens, to climb up the steps of the little chapel which seemed to serve no useful purpose ever, and I could not imagine the sound of hymns pouring out from that dry, uninteresting interior.

I loved to reach Gyllyngvase Beach over the line of rocks, grey and polished by successive tides when the decorum of a quiet walk would be replaced by a series of leapings across or slithering or climbing or crunching over a stony inlet. As I said, this stretch of shore was not our own. I remembered it because of an incident which became more sinister as I grew older. On a hot day, sitting under a concavity of the cliff, was a red-faced man with a handkerchief over his head and he was lying back, not as the holiday makers or Falmouth 'beaching parties' would lie; his trousers were opened and pulled down. He called me over to see more closely something, which even from a distance filled me with fear and distaste. I never walked on this part of the shore after that.

Gyllyngvase Beach was more significant; it was the beach for the 'visitors'; there were bathing huts and a café which sold ice cream, and the raft, a bouncing, solid square which floated at just the right swimming distance from the shore. Cousin Frank, who played water polo for Falmouth, and his cronies made this their venue.

These frail childhood memories were deepened as later, adolescent experiences turned the café into a winter stage, empty except for myself and a boyfriend or fellow nurse from the Royal Cornwall Infirmary where I was to do my nursing training during the war; the chairs would be upturned on laminated table tops, the bare boards would not be splattered with sand or marks of wet feet, the scene outside would be flecked with sea-spray and grey and we would have entered the deserted building to escape from the cold. And another, more mysterious spot, not noticed at the time by that energetic child, which had somehow become associated with a pre-existence and was to become a place of pilgrimage.

At first I stepped up on to the slight mound as any other child might do. I felt the movement of air or birds or growing in the green background, but I looked seawards. After this it became a habit, repeated on each walk as was the dutiful climb up to the entrance of that small, useless chapel. Was it because of this repetition, merely a childish habit which became ingrained, or was there an influence from the earth and the stones that had a more profound effect? Later I remained mystified by those spiritual moments when I stood on the little prominence, not even meditating, just feeling.

Always at that lively age there was the wheeling and circling, the running and returning to the basic centre of the walk and the quick passing of the civic gardens near the end of the promenade which were filled with summer bedding plants and could never have the exotic fascination of Gyllyngdune Gardens. Along a narrow walkway and at last there was Swanpool which seemed to be the end of Falmouth. This was a large expanse of water around the edge of which we circled. Here there were people from the large houses from Arwenack Avenue and Marlborough Crescent, dressed in Sunday clothes, sauntering with elegance. Carefully treading over uneven patches, watching, perhaps even enjoying, although we could never have guessed, the bullrushes through which the white swans glided, the tumbledown cottages, the different smells of farmland which wafted down from the surrounding hill and the path on the opposite side which led to the wilder and often stormy Maenporth.

Above the floor with the five bedrooms and a stained glass lavatory was an attic which was divided into two rooms. Even in the attic the rooms were quite nice and through the small windows we could see over the grounds of the Falmouth Hotel, a line of palm trees which might have been planted in a desert, and the sea beyond. Each room had a double bed on which was a lumpy feather mattress. These rooms had a dusty mysterious appeal for us which was different from the main bedrooms underneath, and were just as exciting even as the room with the four-poster bed where Grandma Jenkins was to spend her last hours, and as full of atmosphere as the front room near the trees where Sylvia, more than myself, was terrified by the hooting of owls.

Uncle Charlie was an undertaker and that is why I recall him best in his working clothes, a dark suit with a starched winged collar which emphasised his large brown eyes. His good features and black hair made him very attractive to us all. He said funny things and there was enough love in him to match the love of his wife. The happiness in their marriage increased the pleasure of those Easter holidays. Mostly I remember him reclining on a couch surrounded by his pets. Boysie, his horrible Pekinese dog, would lie across his knees; the rabbits could hear music from the wireless through the open window; Felix, the black and white cat, would sit opposite him as close as he dared to the Pekinese dog; the canary swung in a cage above him; and Polly the parrot sat on her perch in her cage on the table. But Polly was Frank's ... Sometimes to keep in with Uncle Charlie I would stroke the Pekinese even though I would be shivering in my sandals, waiting for the growl and the snap.

Polly was transformed whenever Frank was around. She would bounce on her perch, squawk, say over and over, 'Who's a pretty girl then, who's a pretty girl then? Pretty Pol. Pretty Pol.' She would nibble with her lethal beak so gently at the perch; spread her wings; extend a grey, scrawny leg and then scratch her head. All this time her eyes seemed to go more orangy. I would watch Frank as if he was a lion tamer with a fierce creature to subdue.

'Come here!' Frank said the first time. 'Give me your hand.' Much as I trusted him I held back. 'Come on, don't be afraid.' He took my hand and placed it right under the black, shiny beak. My face became still as Polly nibbled my hand; it was a gentle nuzzle, almost as if she were kissing me, and I saw the spread of her wings, the same as she spread them when Frank stroked her. She bounced her head up and down to indicate even more pleasure, then Frank placed his hand under those grey, lizardy claws and brought her out of the cage. Another time it was, 'Come on, let's go down to the beach.' We would go down to the beach and skim stones really far out to sea, especially when it was calm and flat. This flattering intimacy ceased when Howard was around. I might not have existed: the two boys had no time for me ... but Howard was not always there and I was. I was there for a long period when the family was moving house in Truro. This was the reason, I discovered much later in life. At the time, I suppose, like all other children, we take life as it comes. Sylvia was too young and Howard was at school. I was pleased to have all this attention from someone in my brother's elite circle; it went to my head a bit, to have Cousin Frank to single me out for attention.

Everyone had gone into Falmouth town to shop and it was the end of the Easter holiday. Frank told Aunt Flo he would look after me; she seemed surprised at his offer but accepted it and we, Frank and myself, were alone in Central House. I wanted to run down to the beach but Frank said 'No.' He seemed to be a bit moody; I wondered if he regretted having taken responsibility for me, but I remained in his shadow, not doing anything which would draw attention and, I thought, his displeasure. He seemed to be restless, moving from one room to another, and I followed. Sometimes he was in the front room and struck a few notes on the piano, then he would be rustling around upstairs or returning to talk to Polly and to make a fuss of her. There was a quiet and empty feel to the house and Frank made sense when he said, 'Let's go upstairs to the attic.' Before he went he was careful to lock all the outside doors. We crept upstairs. I had a sense of expectation; I suppose his excitement communicated itself to me. It was as if we were on an important venture.

He was leading me by the hand. We reached the attic and looked out of the small window, over the back kitchen roof and towards the sea.

'Let's lie down.' There was a funny sound in his voice and I could not think why he would want to lie on the lumpy bed in the middle of an afternoon. Nevertheless, I went with him to the furthest bedroom and we lay under the shabby coverlet. I could feel Frank's heart thumping. For the first time I felt as if I was ... special ... in another class, almost superior to Frank himself.

There was nothing nasty for me to remember, only that, as he had guided my hand into the parrot's cage, now he was guiding my hand over every part of his body. His hand was warm as he closed his fingers over my own, which was not at all questing. And that was all! No big deal like it was when I went up to Polly's beak. Nothing else for me to remember except that I reported the incident to my Mother when we were settled in the new house. I told the tale with enormous pride and with, probably, generous exaggerations, for visits to Falmouth stopped for a long while ... until everyone forgot.

Falmouth, even in memory, was fascinating: there were so many aspects. Our starting point was always the Arch, just in front of the entrance to the Falmouth Hotel; from here we might choose to walk around Castle Point or along to the Sea Front or we would walk towards the old part of Falmouth, a tiring walk on shopping days when all the bags were full and heavy and Mother and Aunt Flo dragged their steps, but so different at other times. To set off and to reach Market Street with shops dark and shining oak, small panes in the windows, antiques and Cornish stone displays; to pass the gaps which reached into the flashing blue of Falmouth Harbour, Fish Strand Quay, Custom House Quay, Prince of Wales Pier; to climb up the 112 steps of Jacob's Ladder, down again and then to climb a second time, when we were young. To set out at Whitsun to the top of Moor Field and the Fair. All these memories augmented in the future years when teenage pleasures superseded our young adventures. Always it was important to enter Gyllyngvase Gardens and to feel the coolness of the area near the sea, carved out of rock with two shell-lined caves with seats, on which we sat, almost as a ritual. We could study the Australian fern which grew from the centre of the quarry-like clearing right up to spread over the top paths. I knew every corner of the gardens.

And I have already described the stone pillar which stood on a grassy mound and the shiver I experienced and the familiarity, the rightness I felt when I stood in that spot.

I knew the shapes of the rocks and gullies and could spring like a sandfly over the stretch of shore from Castle Beach to Castle Point. The rusty submarines were lumpy; they lay like brown crocodiles in 'The Gullies.' They have since been removed, but for years they were relics of World War 1 which made a dangerous playing arena for the children of our generation who swam in and out of the nailed doors like sardines. There was Jumper's Rock (our name). These grey masses of rock were at the corner of Castle Beach and, as I have said, it was our fearful practice to jump from one point to another. It was a feat which took all of my young, heedless courage which the older self would never attempt.

My sister and I played for long, sunny stretches in the soft, seaweedy pools; bloodsuckers and limpets and little tiny sea creatures we saw, but never, never Christopher Crab.

My Father, whenever he was able, was our companion. With a panama hat and his trouser legs rolled up he searched as hard as we did. He was the solid pivot around which our family revolved quite happily. His vitality remained throughout his life and whenever something was happening, it might be a walk or a swim or just an effort to take a photograph, he showed an interest. And if he was the companion, Mother was the reporter. After an outing to the pictures to see Janet Gaynor or Norma Shearer, or after a day trip to Plymouth, Mother would come up to the bedroom door.

'Are you awake, girls?'

She would open wardrobe doors and cupboards to put away her outdoor clothes, then the door of our bedroom would open. Downstairs Father would be getting the supper.

'Come on, Mabel,' he'd call.

'Just a minute, Will.'

She would sit on the edge of the bed and recount the day's happenings, every detail of the outing, the picture, the train journey, what there was to eat and whoever was there and what they were wearing; she was tireless. Father's voice was now to be heard from the hall downstairs, more impatient, and we girls would say, 'Oh Mum, let's go to sleep ...' But the stories went on until supper was ready.

Though we might have sounded unappreciative, our family did share experiences and right throughout our lives together we had an easy, caring relationship ... Mother's stories helped in this.

I have the tattered copy of her book still, the book which was our alternative to a video or cinema or magic lantern or any future audio or visual entertainment. This book was the centre of my mother and her sisters' childhood and I puzzle often as to how it came into their keeping. Was it perhaps a book that their beloved Auntie brought with her from her period as a companion with Frances Havergail at Plymouth or was it found in a drawer of a cabinet that Granfer happened to be altering? My Mother treasured it I know and I think that of all the sisters she was the one who hankered most after some knowledge that she knew was beyond her reach. And as our mother she fed our own imaginations with her readings from the book ... about small boys who were run down by wild horses or a young couple sheltering each other from a stampede of wild buffalo or a missing soldier or a bride lost whilst playing a game of hide and seek on her wedding day only to be found, years later, in an empty trunk ... a skeleton in a wedding dress.

There were poems from forgotten authors, for instance, the 'Spinning Wheel Song':

Mellow the moonlight to shine is beginning.
Close by the window young Aileen is spinning,
Bent o'er the fire her blind Grandmother, sitting,
Is crooning, and moaning, and drowsily knitting.

Or 'The Whistler' by Robert Story, or 'The Galley Slave' by Henry Abbey. There were lesser-known poems by better-known authors. The book is packed with Victorian emotion, drama and comical recitations: its original purpose was to provide material for students of elocution! I could not tell the name of the book because the cover is missing but it is a book which I would ask to have with me should I ever land on my desert island.

Mother would not be satisfied until our eyes were streaming with tears, then she would close the book gently and allow us to sleep ... perchance to have nightmares.

But that belongs to the Truro part of the story.

****** ****** ****** ****** ******

Uncle Charlie's mother, Grandma Jenkins, sat in the Wireless Room with Aunt Myrtle, her daughter who was nearly as old as herself. She sat and looked at everything and everyone. Her face was hard and frowning ... she was always there.

I never went near her room when I knew they were in and neither did anyone else, even Uncle Charlie. She was a large woman who wore long black skirts and choker blouses. This memory was imprinted on my mind by the large studio portrait of her which was forever in its place on the wall above the fireplace. Poor Aunt Myrtle had a nose which seemed to have been planed down so that it had a blunt smooth end. If I made a noise or ran or broke a piece of cake to eat before I was meant to, it was 'Sshh! ... Grandma Jenkins will have you.' She kept a cane in her room which she said she had when Charlie was a boy, and as she told me this she swished it hard down on the leather sofa head. She never smiled. When she was living at Central House, the middle bedroom with the four-poster bed was hers. I went in with Aunt Flo once when she was making beds and afterwards a picture remained in my mind of white starch, draped dusty curtains, china ornaments and old shoes.

They, the grown-ups, were out on this particular day, everyone except Aunt Flo who was rattling dishes in the back kitchen. I went into the Wireless Room and was attracted by the bell-like, red and blue fuchsia plant. Grandma Jenkins had set this on the centre of her table and indeed, it was the centre of her life ... no one was allowed to touch it.

I climbed on to the table and 'plopped' one or two of the flower heads. The noise was perfect and so was the feel; I carried on until, over-reaching, I slipped and found myself looking down at a fair sized piece of the plant.

There I was; there was the plant and there was the cane. No one came at that moment to see me try to pin the piece back to the whole. I did manage this but the red fuchsia, wounded, sagged like a broken bird's wing. I went upstairs and struggled into my hat and coat and walked out of the house, as I thought, for ever.

Opposite Central House was the Cab Rank where the horses and cabs waited their time between the incoming trains at the station. The station was not far away, just out of sight and up the road. Like all children we liked this spot and watched the cabmen often when they gave their horses oats mixed with chaff in green, canvas nosebags.

I went up to the first cabman and said, 'I want a cab please.'

'Oh, my little maid, and where are 'ee going to?'

'To London.' At the time it must have seemed far enough away.

'Oh. Oh.' He said this and looked at me carefully. 'Right we are then. Jump up.'

He helped me into the leathery cab and closed the door and then climbed up outside to gee up his brown horse. I heard the clip clop ... clip clop, and settled down. We went along the road for a short while and then he turned and brought me back to Central House where he called out for Aunt Flo.

On reflection I think she was as frightened as I was, but between them all, Uncle Charlie included, I was saved from the feared retribution.

****** ****** ****** ****** ******

40

Central House and Christopher Crab
Return

I thought this was the house where I could be certain to find the ghosts of childhood. Central House with its four sitting rooms. The house which we felt belonged to us more than our own and which should have had a more evocative name.

This was the house where Aunt Flo lived with her Charlie and Frank; where summer visitors walked sandal-footed and seemed to have, always, fresh red sunburned faces; where winter 'permanent' lodgers talked and joked by the firesides in the cold months, each having his own corner. I thought I could hear the hollow, mellow notes from the Chappel piano as Frankie vamped his musical way through 'Underneath the Arches' and 'Lily of Laguna' and, of course, 'Wonderful Amy'. On the sun-shining-through landing where each bedroom door led to its own secret life I thought surely one ghost might walk, even if it was only Grandma Jenkins who had died in her four-poster bed. No ... perhaps it would be in the room where Sylvia hid from the sound of the hooting owls, but here we shouted and played and there Aunt Flo made us laugh so much at her stories, no ghost could walk with sufficient decorum and dignity. Perhaps Christopher Crab might rattle small chains behind him on the way to the beach. We might have expected a ghost in the attic, though never in the back bedroom where we slept four in a bed during the height of 'the season' or failed to sleep because of giggling.

So many times I thought I could write of the spirit who must haunt Central House, but there was nothing. Not when Uncle Charlie died whilst on a visit to Truro, nor when Frankie was lost, believed killed, whilst flying with the R.A.F. during World War 2. His diary, which was sent back with his personal things, told of the excitement over his visit to the Garden of Gethsemane. There were some photographs and a few details of his last weeks. Poor Frank and Polly the parrot and Boysie, only scratching sounds and rustles ... no ghosts.

On the day of Aunt Flo's funeral when the snow wind whipped the palm trees in front of the Falmouth Hotel into very non-tropical, bending shapes and I walked past them, through the gap which we had sneaked through, so often, as children, a short cut to the beach, I thought I saw summer geraniums and I leant against the wooden fence over Castle Beach, just breathing in the salty seaweedy smell. This was no smell for ghosts: it was almost too strong, from the black, bladder-wracked rocks, for the living.

Against the green, soft-covered rocks which the waves washed and stroked there was a mist; just where the sand was coarse and brown I saw them. At first the mist swirled round and spread and then there was a

41

CENTRAL HOUSE FROM THE FALMOUTH HOTEL

group forming in its centre. Old-fashioned dresses were on the women and the men were dressed in their flannel shirts with dark trousers. The children in vest-like bathing costumes ran between the sea and the spread tablecloth with its sandwiches and saffron cake. I heard as plain as plain, voices ... shouts ... laughter, the sort of laughter that echoes until the first darkness becomes night.

I stayed until the lights behind me began to go out and it was time to return to the warmth of my room in the Falmouth Hotel where I had arranged to have Aunt Flo's funeral tea so that she could enjoy it.

My ghosts did come to me, bringing the happiness they had known.

CHAPTER FOUR

Across the Harbour

Here was another world which was lit by that special Cornish light and, at night, shone under a yellow saffron bun of a moon. On the quayside the smell of salt pervaded and further out, where the harbour curved round into the sea, the scent was from exotic flowers. On those perimeters lived our old-time jet-setters who put down their pears and peaches, orchid and azalea roots. At the castle end, however, there were some older houses inhabited by more established wealthy people. The new rich never learned that though they bought land and built white, stretching buildings, they remained always on the outside. They would never enter the real world where tough, brown fishermen ranged against them with their oily and native arrogance.

Over the long road which bordered the whole of the harbour from Castle Point to Roseland Point, over the straggle of cottages, mellow houses to the right and large, all-shaped bungalows and houses on the left, over the wash of tide supporting the small boats and yachts outside, an old lady watched who might have been the queen of St Mawes. This was Old Mother Pascoe from the Gerrans and Portscatho area, who had migrated years ago all the way across the Percuil waters.

She had her vantage point, one of the cottages, thatched, at the top of a wide cobbled series of shallow steps which led to the walls of the harbour. She watched, she shrieked her orders and kept to her own style of wearing dark skirts and boots from a former era. Sometimes she lapsed into fragments of the old Cornish language; however, this was imperceptible to local ears, because the dialect in St Mawes contained more close derivatives than most of the other Cornish towns. Her face was brown, tough like a leather pad, and seemed to skew around her little mouth. She reigned, even though she swayed in strong winds and had to hold on to whatever was handy. She had a sharp tongue and most people tried to avoid her tirades. What gave her best in these encounters was that most often she spoke the truth ... the things they would rather not hear.

On the shale path outside her cottage she kept her eye on the world. Near the Castle the road was darkened by older shrubs, there were more shadows and the clean white walls of the cottages showed through with their oak doors and polished brasses which followed the uncluttered lines some of these sea captains had practised at sea. Under the walls across the road in the gardens reaching down to the sea grew exotic plants in their sheltered-from-seawind positions. This southern aspect caught warmth from every available ray of sunshine. Cosseted plants and established, like the people in the houses ... used to the best, used to giving their best and being the best. Not like the flamboyant influx of new people on the other side in their spreading buildings of pink stucco with areas of glass facing the sea. Those who were used to the sea had small windows, easy to shutter in the winter. Apart from the inhabitants there was a shifting, seasonal group of people, real 'toffs'. The Prince of Wales, they say, had a yacht anchored outside and famous stars, Gracie Fields amongst others, and their guests walked the summer street, shopped for goods unheard of by local shopkeepers, in the stores. They were a glamorous group. Trousered women with bright lipstick and loud voices shattered the balmy air with theatrical accents. Someone like Uncle Joe, a character, an old salt able to crew in a sailing race, useful as a contact, was tolerated.

He tolerated them because they paid well.

St Mawes was therefore a mixture of people and their cultures. To belong, one had to be Cornish or a character or to be at home on a sailing boat. Uncle Joe passed on all counts and his failures were ignored ... sly charm being his forte.

****** ****** ****** ****** ******

Aunt Delia's dreams revolved around her Whitsun Fair; Mother's thoughts were lit by her imagination: her longings for self-expression were quenched by a sense of inferiority. She saw Father's family as stiff and lacking in humour. On the other hand she was not as warm as Aunt Delia nor as sharp as Aunt Flo. She was able to pity poor Gertie and could use this sister as a sad kind of heroine on whom she could ponder and pity. Through her, at that time and in the years which were to come, we could trace Aunt Gertie's story.

****** ****** ****** ****** ******

The lively brown-eyed gardener called at the kitchen door every night at six o'clock. It was the time when the activity, all the carving of meat and dishing-up of vegetables, the stoking of fires and stirring of pots, meant he could merge into the background where he could sit by the cupboard in a corner to watch mounds of his own produce being piled into the best dinner service. His own, more humble platter, yet with a king-size helping on it, would be placed in front of him with a jug of tea. This would be enjoyed by him until the bustle subsided.

The girls laughed at his sly repartee which was guaranteed to put Cook in her best mood. The pretty girls tossed their heads and flung their bodies as they passed and the shy ones lowered their gaze before his quick, merry eyes. Gertie was one of the latter and, as it was quoted later, by Mother about her sister, 'She married him, he didn't marry her.'

The upstairs-downstairs life was exciting enough to bring in her sisters and their boy friends. They could all tell the story of the time Aunt Gertie arranged a picnic on the well-kept lawns of her 'Big House' when the Master and Mistress were in Truro for the day. They were entertaining some students from the Camborne School of Mines and these they wanted to impress. A white damask tablecloth, shining with starch, was laid across the grass, fine china and cutlery was placed beside the plates of ham, Hog's Pudding (a real delicacy in Cornwall), hot pasties and sausage rolls of course, and splits and jam and cream. Suddenly the girls who were listening for the sound heard a distant clop clop of a trotting pony and in front of the young men's amazed eyes the feast was whipped out of sight and they, themselves, were rushed out through the back gardens. Just in time, for Old Man Butler and his good lady had returned from their airing.

As we were told and sometimes discovered for ourselves, Roseland was a remnant of pagan country, the last stronghold of the Celts where the customs and language remained that much longer than anywhere else. And it was here that once upon a time Mother's third sister, our Aunt Gertrude, lived with her newly married husband Uncle Joe, the gardener with the quick brown eyes, in a corner of the woods near St Anthony. This part of their lives can well be imagined. It was a perfect place as they both worked on the same estate.

As a gardener Uncle Joe was successful: he was employed as long and as often as he wanted for all of his life. Aunt Gertie applied as much as she possibly could the skills she had learnt during her apprentice years. The good china pieces she had been given as wedding presents were used when she entertained; there were little touches her old Cook had taught her, such as how to make her sponges rise and which herbs to grow in her garden to give her soups and stews a flavour which was only hers. She applied the professional touches and yet made homely fare seem more delicious than anything which could have been bought in the town shops.

Every time I think of my Aunt Gertie she is using her arms and hands. She is beating up eggs or stirring a mixture as she prepares food. She is hanging up clothes or scrubbing; she is winding the handle of the mangle or shaking out mats. All the time she is struggling to make the home attractive to her now-proving-wayward husband. A wooden cupboard with a glass front was given prominence in her best room and glittered with white fluted china with touches of dark blue and gold.

I see a small woman, clean in her print dresses, with her arms dipped in a steaming barrel outside the back door of the cottage or pegging out clothes on the lines which stretched from one tree to an iron ring fastened to the wall of the cottage. I do remember her resting sometimes when she took us down to the smooth rocks above the lapping gullies of the river shore where we ate her home-made buns and rabbit pasties. Uncle Joe caught fish and snared the rabbits which provided food for the table and sport for him.

The passion they shared was an intense respect for the gentry, the old Cornish county people who knew how to treat their servants because, as they both emphasised, they were people who were used to being served. These, they acknowledged as their superiors.

So one can imagine what it was like in those idyllic first days of their early marriage spent in the corner of the woods behind the silver waters of the River Fal. Gertie was pregnant and Joe was the one man in her life. All the work there was to do around the home and the cottage garden she did with every bit of her heart and strength.

Even the effort entailed by the need to row across the water to St Mawes for the weekly shopping did not deter her. Only an inevitable loneliness, perhaps, an increasing disillusionment, against which she fought so much ... and she did fight hard.

The story is remembered even now, by some of the older inhabitants of St Mawes, how on a particular afternoon Gertie set off in her rowing boat to cross the width of the River Fal, between Woodbridge and St Mawes. On this day, the waves were fierce enough to keep most of the fishermen ashore. The men grouped on the quay to help her, holding the boat close to the steps and passing down her cardboard boxes of bacon and flour, Blue Cross matches and Woodbine cigarettes, cheese and all the other commodities necessary for a few weeks of living in their cottage.

The boat bobbed up and down and beat against the steps. One man said, 'Who d'you think you are, Gert ... Grace Darling?'

'I've got Joe's tea and his fags,' she answered as she crammed down her old black 'tam' and set to with the oars in her indefatigable arms. Their warnings were unheeded, and the stubborn will of the little woman prevailed.

Joe was free like the wild animals or the seagulls. He could go out to one of the visitors' elegant and expensive yacht; he'd find some excuse. He could go down to Place House. He could slip across to St Mawes for a drink or team up with a mate on his fishing boat and disappear somewhere amongst the other craft in the Carrick waters. He gardened in some of the big houses which bordered the edge of the river and everyone said he was a good gardener. Sometimes he would bring home a couple of peaches which would have dropped off the back of a lorry if there were lorries in those days. He would present these to my aunt as if they were a bouquet of roses and she would forgive everything. In Summer he spent most of his time crewing for the visiting yachtsmen who vied with each other for his expertise on their sailing ships. He was one of the most sociable of men and was as entertaining to his own cronies as to those who hired him. He was as elusive as an eel and a handful.

It was inevitable that the isolation and perhaps Aunt Gertie's desolation proved too much for them and the bright lights of St Mawes, the picturesque fishing village opposite St Anthony, promised all the sophistication they required. They rented one of the cottages up the cobbled steps behind the harbour which happened to be next to Old Mother Pascoe.

****** ****** ****** ****** ******

Mother told me the truth. Gertie was lonely and frightened. During the first World War there were soldiers camped on the headland at St Anthony and on the nights when Joe was out on one of his innocent fishing expeditions or on some other more mischievous pursuit she crouched inside the walls of her home listening to the boots of passing soldiers as if she were in an occupied country.

'It wasn't as if they meant any 'arm. They was only boys just joined up, like your father, and they never molested her or anything but Gertie thought the worst. In the end she told Joe and he said, "Well, me dear, the only thing is you must come out with me." So he took her out with him in the boat at nights. Well, one night a great big fish came near the boat when they were near Black Rock and tipped it up and Gertie was in the water, nearly frozen she was, until Joe righted the boat and pulled her back in. She was cold like ice and always after whenever the wind turned she was colder than anybody else ever was.

'Course, the upshot of all this was the delivery time of her child came on quicker than it should have been and they had to go back to Devoran where Joe's people were for her to be looked after.' Mother would always draw a big breath at this stage.

'And then a strange thing happened. She had twins. Course, they do run in our family. The first baby that came out had the tail of a fish where his legs should have been. And that's true for you. Mind, the second one came and he was perfect. And that was Charlie.'

****** ****** ****** ****** ******

They moved over to the mainland.

Mother Pascoe had pre-knowledge of them and knew more about Gertie than Gertie did herself.

She greeted the young married woman with a voice which sounded full of wonderment. 'To think I should live to see this day.

'I knew all about 'ee, my dear ... I was there when the storm crashed that boat on the rocks out at Gerrans and your grandfather, he was only a boy, a little lad he was ... about four year old, tied to the piece of mast, was washed up. The captain's son he was. His mother was saved too and she had a velvet bag full of gold coins and jewels. She paid the folks at Gerrans well for the care they took of them. Afterwards she went up the river to Truro or thereabouts where she had a cousin or some other relation.'

This old lady was like a captain on a bridge gazing with her long spyglass out over the waters with intense concentration. She swayed her body to follow the track of the boat and then there was a drawn out 'Ah ... ah.' She seemed to be satisfied. She was watching the small-as-a-fly speck which was moving towards the shelter under the Idle Rocks.

The younger women in their doorways watched, laughing and chattering amongst themselves. The old lady, grey hair straggling from her cloth cap and in her long black skirts, was a bit outlandish after all, and when they were together they felt strong enough to stand up to her.

'Well, old Hawk-eye,' Aunt Gertie said, 'what's the latest today?'

The other women giggled. 'What are they having for dinner out on the lighthouse?'

'Hawk-eye! If I had a spare one I'd give it to 'ee. If anybody wanted another one ... to watch that man of yourn.' She waved her spy-glass towards an ivy-covered cottage just up past the Roseland Hall.

The women became quiet and looked with anxiety towards their neighbour. This was something they had all discussed over their cups of tea. 'They're always the last to know,' they had said. And Old Mother Pascoe was always right.

Aunt Gertie's eyes, grey and large like her twin-sister Delia's, lost their light. They widened and always afterwards she had a strained, mournful look. She became involved with the Church. The ladies of the village praised the way she scrubbed the floors, starched the altar cloths and polished the stout pieces of oak in the pews. Her body was bowed with her efforts and she became smaller and smaller as the years passed. Later they moved to Glebe Cottage on the corner of the steep hill down to the harbour.

And this, I suppose, was where my own St Mawes life began.

I was old enough now to be part of the community which was clannish enough to exclude most new-comers. We stayed often enough in the old part of the village to be accepted. Aunt Gertie would say, 'Run down to the quay and tell Joe that supper is ready.' I would go down the short hill and in summer dusk hear the plash of water and a gentle creak of oars.

My shrill voice carried across the harbour. 'Uncle Joe ... Supper.'

I'd call again, 'Aunt Gertie says "Come on in to supper."' Then the reply, the string of sailor abuse rattling back, the gist of it being that my voice was disturbing the fish.

At times he would wake us early in the morning to walk the fields behind the castle to search for mushrooms. Once when I had walked the wet grass for nearly two hours without finding a mushroom and not calling out in case he shamed me with his full basket and mocking comments, I discovered it was the same with him. No matter! With three mushrooms between us he rowed me out to his fishing boat and his cronies and with the mackerel they caught and a fresh brew of tea, we enjoyed a meal never to be forgotten.

Once, when he returned from his fishing in the early hours with a good catch, he got Aunt Gertie to fry them right away and made certain 'they maids' were dragged out of bed to ' 'ave a taste.' Only afterwards we laughed: Sylvia and I were far too sleepy at the time.

The table ran the length of the kitchen under the window. Chairs on the side were backed to the wall and on one of these, or nearly two, Minnie sat, moving a little so that her arms were free to manipulate the trumpet which kept her abreast of any scandal. Mary Hitchens, tall and as broad as a Scots hammer thrower, settled next. Her face was wind-brown and as lined as any fisherman's. A few younger neighbours took their places. The young married women had time to themselves when their husbands were out fishing. They were glad to be included in such kitchen gatherings. They must have learnt a lot.

A large iron kettle, always blackleaded to a dull shine, was placed on a hotter part of the stove and soon all latent steam hissed out of the spout. Expectant faces turned towards Aunt Gertie. The opening line, 'What's on down the Quay?' was ritual before they chatted on homely things, about their fishermen husbands, boats and shoals of fish past Black Rock. A recurring theme, taken with anxiety or pleasure, but with seriousness, was the weather. Winds and rain were their business. Gertie's arms kept returning to the flour in the bowl. I can see those strong skinny arms with fingers flexible and sure working as she rubbed in yeast and lard. Once the dough was set aside she made the tea. The sugar dish on a stand, milk jug, cups and saucers were laid and after a while, tea, brown and dark as ale poured from the clome tea-pot. Hands reached for cups.

'You always make a good cup of tea, Gert.' And it was the strongest, sweetest tea that I ever remember. If I came up the salt damp passage too early and if I interrupted one of the more classified of these sessions, Aunt Gertie would say, 'Have you seen Joe?' Whatever the answer I would be sent back down the hill to the quay for a pound of butter or a loaf of bread, or to complete some other errand.

I would have liked to stay to hear the latest about Shanghai Lil, the girl who lived with her father and brothers and sisters half-way up Roseland Hill. One on her own, they said, who met the last steamer every night, they said. They whispered things like, 'We don't know if it's her father or her husband.' Or, 'Never mind how many rooms there are, they all sleep in the same bed.' The most urgent warning, 'Don't let me hear you maidens have been talking to her.'

Shanghai Lil. An exotic name to surround with a romantic aura the scraggy girl with black hair who lived in the cream coloured cottage, half-way up Rose Hill. She never spoke to us, never mixed with the older girls of our age, the tough wild daughters of the working community. She was a wraith with greasy locks, seen as she moved from the quay when the steamer came in, or on the slopes of the hill. Sometimes she paused, as everyone paused, to lean over, to embrace the harbour wall. Her face was pale and there were shadows under her large eyes.

I had to see where she lived. 'Trash!' my aunt said so many times.

I trudged up Roseland Hill. There was the small, thatched cottage. My aunt was right, I could not miss it. Roseland Hill was a steep, narrow lane, and the hedges grew out profusely and crawled with honeysuckle. Just in the foreground of the cottage children played. I noticed they had no shoes on their feet and the ends of their skinny legs were bare. Their faces were smudged with toffee or mud; it made no difference which: the substance had dried and blended with the brown of their faces. Every now and then one began yelling and would run into the house. In the porch, as though on guard, a man sat on a kitchen chair. When a child tried to pass him, it was cuffed and sent back into the road to play. I slowed my footsteps so that I could study the scene. I wanted to take in as much as I could; some instinct told me that if I declared an interest there would be scant welcome.

I saw Lil in the background and I knew the girl saw me because she withdrew her black eyes and lowered her head. As though she wanted to stave off any contact she came out and looked fearfully between myself and her father. I might have said something if she had been on her own; curiosity, I suppose, or the fascination with something evil.

Now, I imagine, the cream walls of the cottage do not flake off on to the cobbled paving; the thatched roof is tidy, the windows are polished and geranium plants brighten the dark interior. Some writer or artist or summer migrant inhabits the cottage on the hill, never appreciating the wealth of dramatic material their presence has erased.

When the gang, clique, gaggle or neighbourly watch had left I was allowed to help clear the table. We washed up the cups and saucers, laid the table for dinner and sat on the chairs to wait for my uncle. A ritual.

Outside the window on a rainy day, the paved yard bounced back the rain and crinkly ferns in old earth beds cupped silver slivers of moisture as if holding diamonds. Empty pails filled and overflowed. But Aunt Gertie stayed in her kitchen and cooked. She liked baking; she liked giving; her famous rabbit pasties, home-made bread, jam sponges and pies were spread on all the shelves and spaces around the kitchen. Her working area was the radius of her arm, from the top of the table to the stove. She drew pots and pans from the pile on the floor near her feet.

Most often I stayed in St Mawes by myself and because I was in the same age-group I knew the local girls quite well. I knew them all, some like Ginger and a few of the Saul girls. The Saul girls had dark straight hair, slim brown bodies in summer frocks, freckles and curls, energy verging into wildness. I was at home in this unruly company.

Our picnics on St Anthony or Molunon followed a pattern. Two or more boat-loads of us with our bathing gear and food would be rowed over the water. We beached like old hands, pulling our boats up over the shingly tide line to be left as we made a camp between the rocks. We changed and our cast-off clothing littered the roughened green rock surface. On spread towels we staked our day's territory. All the extra vitality was expressed in shouts of laughter and in dashes into the deep bladder-wracked water, in swims out to the crinkled, grey, roughened water outside the curve of the inlet. Back to the beach, brief spells in the sun, climbs to the green path towards the lighthouse and St Anthony.

When the sun lowered and the air cooled and some of the energy lessened, we packed remnants of food, the primus and kettles, washed cups in the tide and stacked them for the next time. A row back across the water. St Mawes Castle, red in the last light, Place House in almost black shade, lights springing from houses behind the Quay. If it was late enough to go home to bed after mooring we were content. My friends called for me at the house with the long passages to row out to St Anthony for a picnic or to walk from end to end of the sea road in the evenings or to make up a team in the regatta races. Summer nights were long. They were filled with teenage activities.

Across the Harbour

In St Mawes, Regatta Day was the big one and we had plans to make. At night dusk had settled over the roofs and chimney-pots but, over the courtyard made up of the square backs of houses, we sat in the open windows and called across to each other.

'Now then you night-crows. Go to bed,' Aunt Gertie called up from her little fern-filled yard with its wooden tubs and tin bath. I took part in all the regatta races when I was eligible and was chosen to be in most of the team games. We spent the day in our swim-suits, laughing, pushing each other into the water when the tide was high, sinking each other's boats after the pram races. Prams were small craft for quick use between boats, similar to the old coracles.

Afterwards we slipped home to dry off and change and watched for the band to assemble on the Quay.

Before the music starts a current of expectation swirls round and through the groups gathered in the road to the castle or to Point and on the Quay. The sun glitters on the brass instruments and the strips of gold on bandsmen's uniforms as the men greet each other before their marathon task. Already they have lost everyday identities. Will, normally gangling and laconic, working as he does, by the stoves in the back of the baker's, looks like a Ruritanian prince. Jim, his butcher's rosy cheeks even rounder, draws deep breaths; Uncle Howard's small dapper figure emerges from the back sitting room of Glebe Cottage which has been the setting for a glorious buffet prepared for members of the village band by the ever industrious women. My uncle's neat business suit is garnished by red and gold and the drums, fastened on to his person, almost eclipse his mild, smiling face. He stands poised, baton held, as the same current of excitement encircles separate sets of villagers and holidaymakers into a thicker, more significant, crowd. From everywhere, out of cottage doors, up the stone steps from the beach, along the road and down the hills, come children. Without being told or directed, they file in couples and form an everlengthening tail behind the, now organised, band. Boom ... boom ... boom ... and the breathing of the crowd becomes deeper, the Floral music, timeless and ever-exciting begins. The heart beat of the Floral Dance ... over and over again ... da da ... di da da da ... la ti ... da di da da ... Was this when the embryo blood cells first became aware or was it before? Does the music vibrate on the branches of trees in Coombe, the stones in our ancient streets or over the choppy waves of our lit Cornish shores? All of us children were led into the streets by the refrain ... la da ... di da da da ... La ... One two three and a skip, through the cool, slabbed passages of the St Mawes or the Ship; through any slipway where the crowd could squeeze, the decorous two-by-two now as undisciplined as a football crowd, only controlled by the insistent and maddening throb. Uncle

Howard, Will, Andrew, and Jim were the spirits of those who served round the fires in primitive rites. Not only children, but young men and women, old men and women were drawn into the fanatical stream. Nothing would stop our pagan caperings. Down the road from the Castle a car, which belonged to the new people, comes. Cars were alien things in those days and had not usurped people on our native roads. The band and the first of the children slowed their pace, but we had not stopped: the music played still and was a compelling force. And then, I remember it to this day, a crowd of young men in their flannels and white shirts, khaki shorts and summer vests, surged around the car ... their multi-muscled arms grasped and lifted, shook and rocked the vehicle. Still moving with the music and almost chanting our tribal dance, we held back. The white-as-a-winnard-faced driver must, with gratitude, remember still how the weight of the car prevented it reaching the height of the wide and bleached walls over which it would have hurtled on to the pebbled Castle Beach.

Always the thrill, each year, it never failed, years later to be remembered: three booming, hollow sounds on the drum and the music of the Floral Dance. Young girls and boys starting with eagerness and light steps, hopping or tripping along the street towards the Castle, crowds filling in behind the band, and it was a moving, heaving mass of reds, yellows, dark blues and little heads like tops of cabbages.

****** ****** ****** ****** ******

A Menacing Companion

Janey lifted her head suddenly, recalling an odd fact. Peggy, whose shoulders were like a speckled brown egg this time of the year, turned towards her, her blue eyes screwed up against the sun and ready to brim over into laughter.

'Don't you see ...?' Janey could not finish. Having pre-knowledge of the joke, she was incoherent.

'Oh come on ...' I said because I knew how long Janey could keep this up.

'Well. We'd be all out of sight, wouldn't we ... under the water.'

Now all of us laughed. The thought of the bird-faced American woman focussing her camera and the excitement in her transatlantic voice as we gurgled with the boat as it went under the water. 'Aw ... how they're gonna love this back home.' And afterwards, as we bobbed up like corks and turned the small boat the right side as we swam and pushed it back to the quay steps, 'Oh my, they're like young newts.'

We could play up to the summer visitors as well as Uncle Joe and the other men. We did not want pints set up in the bar but were satisfied with the one-upmanship. They had their up-the-country accents and smart holiday clothes and we ... well, we had our identity. Blue evening gloss under the wall of the Quay and steps warm and slippery to sit on or to use as a diving point. We had access to several skiffs and providing we moored tidily at the end of the day we had the freedom of the harbour.

To-day, for example, we had just come back from St Anthony Beach. Our boat was stained pink from foxglove petals and still a bit heavy with salt water. We had to bale like mad coming back, because the submerging on the beach did nothing to swell the woodwork. It had not been staunched since last year we were told.

I noticed old Misery Brown was in his usual spot. Last night and the night before he watched us, not laughing indulgently like the locals or treating us with avid admiration like the visitors. Sometimes holiday strangers acted as if they would buy us to put on the mantel shelves back home beside the brass pixies. He might not have been so old. Just that his face was white and his hair thin and he had old-fashioned spectacles which we had seen in the backs of old cupboards, discarded by our parents. We so named him because he never smiled and he wore a shirt which was the exact colour of his dark, sun-burned face.

We lay back in the boat like miniature whales and it rocked with our laughter.

Summer was like this, always. Everyone was out in the evenings and no one seemed to go to bed. That is why, even now at eight o' clock, I knew there would be plenty of time to leave the others, go over the Castle fields to St Just in Roseland and back to the chip shop which was our rendezvous.

Our dry clothes were in bundles under the windlass on the quay where we had left them and we changed quickly in spite of our changing room being the platform of the quay steps. Now, feeling dry and warm in my red velvet pants and sweater, I waved to the others and sauntered off. I knew they would guess where I was going. Occasionally they came with me, but I never asked them especially. They did not share my need for solitary moments.

The fields had been cut and the stubble jabbed like sharp bamboos between the thongs of my sandals. Funny, this was the sort of pain I liked. For the length of the whole field I wondered why this should be. It was less anguish than the longing and yearning which made me almost sick as in this moment when I reached the top of the rise and could see the dark blue harbour water with lively sailboats like butterflies, the border of a thick green band of trees and fields and then the outer, more misty, pale blue rim of the English Channel. It was awful ... no, frightening ... powerful ... no, overwhelming.

But today I smiled as I remembered all the funny things and wondered how long it would be before we were too grown up for such antics. Our mothers thought that at nearly seventeen we should be much more ladylike. I turned once when I heard footsteps and noticed the old man on the quay was taking the same walk.

I had never noticed him away from the quay before, or the children's park outside the Roseland Hall. Still, everyone could enjoy the scenery. Just now when I looked behind he stopped and was engrossed in the view past Castle Point to the open sea. It could be he was taking a constitutional. His presence, however, spoilt my evening. I suppose I am selfish, liking to be lonely sometimes and not wanting anyone else to share, well even the same air. I thought if I walked over the fieldpath to the small wood I could let him pass me before I actually went down to the old river bank. I could not bear him near me there.

My walking was mechanical now and for a while I concentrated on the path in front of me. I did not stop even at the white gate which gave a small framed picture of the harbour. I just thought hard on the plan to let 'Old Misery Brown' out of my evening. Perhaps it would not take too long. He seemed to be walking much quicker now. I could hear, although I was a bit nervous of looking, that he was closer behind me.

I made up my mind that he must pass. It was becoming monotonous, the steady crackling of his footsteps, one-two-three-four, not like the rhythm of marching, lighter and a little quicker, but still, too determined.

I was close to the trees now and could see how thickly the honeysuckle grew. I wanted to stand quiet to absorb the scent which was wasting in the evening. His steps spoiled all this. I dawdled a little and kept my eyes away from him and hoped that his steps would snap right past me.

Suddenly everything sounded quiet. As though I was a field creature I had a prickling sensation which warned me of danger ... right down the middle of my back. The silence was drastic because it was linked with my breathing which for a moment or two had become almost impossible. I could not move my legs or body and could not turn my head. I had never seen his face at close quarters yet I knew exactly what he would be like. I felt his hand grasp my arm and he pulled me round like a limp doll to face him.

I stared into his dry brown face, into his eyes, misty and fixed behind his wire framed spectacles. His mouth was open and I could see spit on the furrow from one corner of lip to chin. It frightened me more because he was trying to smile.

Now that he had turned me, he caught his other hand round my left arm and I was held fast. The funny thing was I couldn't scream. My mouth was as dry as burnt cloth. His face was large and grotesque as he pulled me nearer to him. I closed my eyes.

He began shaking me. Small furious shakes like a terrier with something difficult to handle.

'Laugh ... laugh.' The unbelievable command made me open my eyes. 'Laugh.' His voice was husky and now had lost the first wildness. 'Like you laughed down there with the young ones ... the boys and girls. Kids like laughing, don't they?' His voice was pleading. 'For me ... just once ... will you?'

Pulling suddenly I dropped down and squirmed out of his hold. The life returned to my legs and I was able to run. Out of the shadow of the trees and on to the sunlit field path which led to the main road. I heard his voice behind me. It called despondently, 'Don't be afraid girl ... don't mind me.'

The road was hard and it was easier to be quick. All thoughts of the river beach went from my mind. To reach the others, to tell them, that was all I wanted. To be able to see their faces, unbelieving. To see Janey and Peggy and Ginger with their incredulous eyes, daring me to go on. Then we would laugh.

I never did laugh though. When I rejoined the others, Janey asked if I had been cold and Ginger said, 'The walk has tired you, hasn't it?'

****** ****** ****** ****** ******

Just Breathing Cornish Air

There were long sojourns in St Mawes and the place is seeped into my whole self. If I ran down to the quay in the morning when the air was clean-washed by salt I could climb up on the wide stone walls just to breathe. In this way I felt the rocks and the Channel, the outer blue beyond Falmouth, the dark corners of Place House becoming part of me. I knew the faces of the men on the boats and the feel of the round wall along the sea road. I knew the exact times of the steamers.

Yes, the slivers of blue sea between green fields, the walks to St Just in Roseland church, the breeze around Castle Point and the scents in the old gardens are as vivid in my mind as when I ran amongst them all. Sometimes, as in Falmouth, I traced the line of the harbour on the shore. I loved the rocks. On Castle Road there were slate steps worked into the

GLEBE HOUSE : ST. MAWES

wall which led to the beach. The last step was steep enough to make people jump. This was where we dug for our copper and silver. Change fell from pockets of visitors and stayed in the shingle, waiting for us.

Glebe Cottage was around the first corner of the hill from the Quay to the back of the village. It was a funny little house with long passages. The lower one smelt of mackerel and its walls were always wet. It led straight into a narrow kitchen where Aunt Gertie washed and baked and held court in the mornings. She had two air holes bored in her kitchen door once, and forever afterwards they had to be covered because she thought they were too much like a pair of eyes. The other passage was carpeted with a worn flower-patterned carpet and led to the front door which was set on the corner of the house. The curve outside this door was cobbled and when the sun shone the house was warm and inviting. The doorway led to yet another passage linking it to the stairs and the back sitting room where the local band held their practice sessions.

I have spoken of the friends and neighbours who were the regulars and who seemed to pour into Aunt Gertie's kitchen from all directions. Big, hatchet-faced Mary from opposite came through the wet passage, and round, lumbering deaf Minnie who had to hold her ear-trumpet aloft as she walked sideways down the top passage came from the next house. And of course, when she was alive there was Old Mother Pascoe.

Uncle Joe was expected to blow in at intervals during the day and if he did not report for a few hours I would be sent down to the quay to see 'what Joe was doing.' One evening I reported with some pride that Uncle Joe was entertaining a group of holiday makers, 'Up-the-country toffs' as he called them, to be distinguished from gentry and his own friends. He was playing a concertina on the quay. An old song, ' There was I, waiting at the gate, waiting at the gate ... Oh how it did upset me.' His feet were stamping and his small black head swayed from side to side. No music-hall audience could have been more enraptured. Aunt Gertie was satisfied with this. My instinct told me not to say if I saw him disappearing through the doors of the Ship and Castle, the Rising Sun or the St Mawes.

Sometimes we went to the 'Pictures' in the new Roseland Hall and had to take hot-water bottles and a blanket each. Sometimes when there was a good fire in the corner sitting room which had two windows giving an excellent view of those coming down the hill to go to church, Aunt Gertie would give a colourful commentary ... 'Here's Ginger, she's got her mother's coat on.'

'Oh look ... Annie's late again.' A tall, thin-faced woman whose hair jutted from a woollen cap swirled around the corner, her arms like flails as she struggled to bring the two sides of her coat together.

'Now they're down to the last and only, 'ere's me 'ead, me arse is on the way to come and they can ring the bell.' This description fitted only too well a young boy who stuck his rump out as he walked.

The front room was thick and square. Arm chairs crushed in corners and the table filled the centre. A large fire banked high over-heated the room whilst Uncle Joe slept off his Sunday dinner or our family on a visit exchanged gossip. The best china, brown-patterned and fluted, was laid on starched and spanking lace. There was apple tart, cream and her special jam-sponge, and always to begin, her thinnest of bread and butter. Uncle Joe grumbled happily about our appetites but afterwards I did wonder just how much these teas had cost.

Aunt Gertie cleaned for the Church, cooked for the Vicarage teas, washed and starched the linen and polished the brass, but I never saw her go to Church, not then. Only once, years later, when there were national prayers for the return of the Dunkirk men on their many boats, we went together. It was a day with a rough wind and she crammed a black tam o'shanter on her head ... no Sunday hat! It was not as if Aunt Gertie disliked the people she mocked; perhaps her wit ran away with her. We laughed because the nasty things she said were apt.

And with Uncle Joe, the merry eyes, still brown, slid into cockiness and later betrayed a slyness which was mitigated by an engaging smile. Those massive fisherman, gardener, jockey shoulders were as expressive as any continental's. I can see them hunched over the round sea wall in excitement over a sailing race; lowered in dejection, framed forward in aggression, lifted to this side or that as he danced or played his concertina. Always their outline was emphasised by his crew-necked, black jersey. His face, brown as teak, smiled at the world. Like a pied piper he was born to lead many women in a dance. Aunt Gertie, his grey-eyed bride who, full of hope, jumped beside him on the trap which left Devoran on their wedding day, was a wraith which haunted the cornered house on the hill. As Mother said often, 'She married him, he didn't marry her.'

When my Mother and Father came down on weekends I felt, from my point of view and from the St Mawes point of view, which I thought I understood, that they were perhaps a little refined in the environment I considered my own. I felt a little awkward when I met my village friends. Uncle Joe treated my Father with great respect, and to prove his high opinion he appeared himself at the meal table on time. Aunt Gertie never failed to produce her best. But this she did at all times.

Father would be taken down to the quay to chat with the older men who spent their days just watching. If there was a cricket match to be played in the Playing Field at the top of the village it was a suitable occasion for all. Cousin Charlie would be one of the leading players and he looked very handsome in white which contrasted with his dark looks, almost Spanish. My uncle was everywhere. He took money at the gate, bringing out glasses of lemonade or helping to carry trestle-tables and benches from one place to another. He wore his last year's steward's badge with pride. My Father's grey-blue eyes screwed up in the sunlight, expressed amusement, but on the whole he acted the part of a visiting celebrity with solemnity, assuming all the dignity which Uncle Joe needed for his own esteem amongst the mixture of inhabitants from the village. Father was 'toff' enough to get by with those who thought they were somebody and responded with genuine courtesy to Joe's own pals. My Father revelled in all this attention.

****** ****** ****** ****** ******

Other Aunts and Uncles

Nothing was ever as important as our staying with our maternal aunts but close contact was kept within the whole of the family. Each Christmas was a time of family parties which each branch held in their respective homes. In those days I recall front rooms with banked up fires which (to me at any rate) did not betray hours of cleaning and work. They just glowed and lit the small rooms with mantelpieces arrayed with china ornaments. The gas light was mellow and lighting up was a ritual. Only down in St Mawes do I really remember the rosy glow of oil lamps. To anyone outside Cornwall our idea of a party meal must seem monotonous. Tea was not anything special without our splits and jam and cream. Suppers meant sausage rolls and small pasties; often there was a plateful of home-cured ham for the adults. In these houses we never stayed overnight, and there was just once when I spent a week with my father's sister Aunt Millicent down at Mabe.

Mabe was a village near Penryn and Falmouth. It was rural but it depended on work from a local quarry for most of the inhabitants. And this is what was strange and perhaps contributed to my never knowing where I belonged in the social structure. I found the working industrial labourer's way of life alien. For example Uncle Harry came home in his working clothes and washed outside in lots of soapy water before coming in for his dinner which was at tea time. He was up so early in the morning that I never saw him at breakfast and he went to bed when all the rest of the family stayed up late to chat by the fire. He was tall and brown with large hands which I can see in my mind's eye grasping the West Briton which he read as he drank his tea at supper time. His Cornish accent was broader than ours but not with as many Cornish sounds prevailing as in, say, Aunt Flo's or Uncle Joe's who both framed sentences in a way that made people laugh. Aunt Millicent was very prim and her house was spotless; she attended all chapel occasions and played her part in the village life and I remember she was so kind to me when I had toothache and had to go to the dentist. But I never was really at home in Mabe. And I never became close to my cousins there, Ronnie and Malcolm and Peggy. Maybe the Wilnor blood ran too strongly in the veins.

CHAPTER FIVE

Years which belonged to Truro

Our young years were eventful because Cornwall lent all its resources to imaginative children. With the benefit of this treasure trove the children could be as extravagant as they pleased and for us, even as small fry, the mainstream of family life flowed as inexorably as small rivers ebbed into the Fal. My uncertainty regarding our place in the social structure remains and Cornish imagination does not change the fact that we were just an ordinary family. Only grandfathers who were drowned at sea or great-uncles who were missionaries and worked in leper colonies or aunts who had mermaids as babies or entertained little men-crabs for breakfast provided a bit of excitement.

The primary schools we attended, Daniell Road School at first from Fairmantle Street, and next Bosvigo, were typical of the time, dreary buildings with oak-blocked floors, smelling of ink and chalk. There were small desks intricately carved with initials and dates, and schoolmasters and schoolmistresses who seemed shiny-suited and middle-aged, and if they were interesting it was because they were too tall or they were fat or they had a wart on the end of their noses. When the big man sat me on his heavy thighs and I saw the white specks of dandruff on his shiny navy suit and he said that he was sorry to have to hit me with the ruler I cried. I wanted to run home to tell my Mother but I knew my brother would be there and feared his laughter. He had not yet tired of repeating one story which proved just how much of a Cornish accent was used in our ordinary conversation. He teased me often about an incident when I described the big moon mentioned by our class teacher, who wore a brown knitted suit all summer and winter, that I thought the moon was 'laughing at we.'

We streamed or straggled from classes to the yard at playtimes, to scream and yell either as tormentors or victims, and always finished at four o'clock, returning to our homes wrapped in warm navy-blue coats and stout shoes. From Bosvigo Primary School we stopped to slide on the muddy splats or to swing round tree trunks which spread out from hedges in Redannick Lane or to search in little cavities in moss or bark which were so fascinating to our young eyes.

Years which belonged to Truro

Just recently, on a Christmas card I received, there was a coloured photograph of Truro which depicted the curve of the street between Redannick Lane and the bottom of Kenwyn Street. There was the shop window of the little shop which sold chitterlings and other offal, especially tripe which looked like the fleece of a lamb. Often things do change, streets disappear, even the old Post Office and Library made a huge hole in the sky-line when I saw a new development for the first time whilst on holiday, but the bones of a place remain. The line of the hills is constant.

Very nearly, once, I attained some distinction by winning a prize for an essay in a competition for all the city's schools. There was a presentation in a local cinema and I was told to attend. I went to the Regent Cinema on my own; sat on top of the swung-back seat on the edge of a row of red upholstered chairs. When my name was called I walked up to the front, received my book even then almost in tears and I stumbled back up the aisle. There were hands and arms reaching out to help me and murmurs of 'This way dear.' 'Over here my love.' But no Mother or Father to watch with satisfaction. So I remember my moment of glory with shame.

My parents regretted this more than myself, I know.

My Father never mentioned the subject - his feelings were too involved to put them into words - but my Mother said so often, 'Oh, to think I never went down with you. I didn't know it was anything like that ... You should have told me.'

Somehow, with natural subtlety, she managed to shift the blame.

****** ****** ****** ****** ******

My Mother was afraid of any of us becoming 'too big for our boots' and both parents were afraid themselves of showing off. Therefore it was inevitable that the three of us children tended to underrate ourselves and just as certain that later we would sell ourselves very short in life's Co-op. We had so much going for us which we did appreciate and we lapped up these good things, the cosy aunts, the laughter, the fun of our holidays which in retrospect seemed to be long blue sojourns in lazy places. Maybe we took the good as well as the not-so-good for granted. When we were older there were the parties following invitations to big houses owned by those we considered to be posh girls in the County School. Today these houses, some of them square and Georgian, imperishable, are just as elegant and just as much a status symbol as the numbers of middle-class citizens increase and the solid structures are divided into roomy flats for the people who can afford them.

We were on the lists approved of by affluent parents just as I was on the approved list for the Regatta races at St Mawes. Mother invited my friends back for our party and in fairness to her she did her best. I dreaded these events, fearful in case I might be embarrassed: at that time Mother's lack of the formal graces could make me cringe. I must have been a little horror for this was my private dread. My friends enjoyed themselves - they were not as inhibited - and when I consider, I think we had as much fun in our house as in any of the others ... perhaps more. Food was never a matter for one-upmanship ... rich or poor, good cooks or bad cooks, party fare was the same as picnic fare and so standard that we knew exactly what to expect ... jelly and cream, splits and cream and jam, sausage rolls and saffron cake ... coconut macaroons. When the man of the house returned from work, party games were organised like Postman's Knock which seemed to have more significance as we got older. The bigger parties were held in a hired room which might be over a Baker's or a Fruiterer's. Although we were old enough it was not a usual thing for us to dance so when a gramophone was hired to provide music it was for games like Pass the Parcel or Musical Chairs.

****** ****** ****** ****** ******

The First Dance

We were sitting on the round, polished chairs along the edge of the floor ... games had become a bit boring. I suppose it was because we were older we were bored with the same old routine of parties with the same faces and we longed for January to be finished.

The man who was in charge of the gramophone moved to the walnut cabinet to change the record. We had been listening to tunes like 'South of the Border', one popular tune at the time. Some of us were tapping our feet and some, the sophisticated, were dancing ... almost ... The record? Something like 'Red Sails in the Sunset' or 'Bye Bye Blackbird', I suppose. He walked over to the corner where I sat with some friends, all of us strange and stiff in cold party frocks, and asked me to dance. I looked around at the giggling faces of my friends where there was no support and I am certain I was blushing when I stood up on the slippery surface (they used french chalk then to make feet slide more easily); waited until his arms caught round me, and the girl who could race like a cat over the seaweed rocks felt as unsteady as if she had only one leg.

But I remember the smell of his coat: it reeked of tobacco which was not a nice mixture with the smell of sweat. I did like the feel of the material though, rough and tweedy, and when I caught hold of his arms to steady myself they were hard and supporting.

The parties we attended most of the times were necessary   social occasions. It would have been the end of our world not to be invited yet there were many other things I would rather have been doing. I suppose there was a little excitement in putting on a special dress, but taffetas and artificial silks felt very cold in the winter months. In those days we did not wear comfortable jeans and tee-shirts as a social uniform.

Yet I did not need this winter social life.   In retrospect it was associated with private anxieties, mostly unrealised.

I would have missed much more a run on the sands or a paddle in the sea or a long climb up all the steps in Jacob's Ladder at Falmouth.

****** ****** ****** ****** ******

Life in the Town

The grey City Hall stood as if it had been slammed together by an army of strong men who intended that it should dominate the town for ever. And it did. Dark grey stonework without embellishment, stone floors, polished in the main hall to make the floor where my father skated and I was to dance to the music of Glen Miller in my teenage years. This is where crowds congregated to buy and sell, to listen to speeches from hopeful candidates for Parliament and to hear the results, to cheer or abuse.   A building as solid as the business community of Truro could desire where they could manipulate the affairs of their city.   It was here in the foyer where at one time stocks were kept, and outside in Boscawen Street people gathered who would mock those being punished and probably throw their tomatoes. I puzzle sometimes on this surfeit of tomatoes ... was the climate much warmer in those days?   It was here in the square outside the City Hall, not Victoria Square which must have been the original Market Square at the bottom of Calenick Street, nor High Cross, where other crowds gathered in later years for all the Cathedral and other municipal parades.   It was in Boscawen Street that the local hunt met with all its pageantry and on a winter's night it was worth our while to join the crowds who jostled outside the City Hall to see the gentry move into the building in their silks and taffetas, their escorts in dignified evening suits.   With experience gained over the years, it is possible to appreciate the wide differences which were between those who were 'up in the world' and others.   My own generation had their special gatherings.   We met and in simple times moved off into the country to the sound of the Floral music, our venue the top of Treyew Road where we played games and had our saffron bun, or

No 2. FAIRMANTLE ST.

on V.E. day or V.J. day when we streamed out to Trewarthenick grounds to dance around a bonfire to celebrate with a pagan delight throughout the night. It was easy to see how the custom of bringing in the May was so ingrained in our blood. The solid thrust of the City Hall which was the Regent Cinema and the Skating Rink and at one time the Market has been background to most of the recent history of Truro.

One could appreciate how this building looms and forces itself on administrative matters in Truro. The buying and the selling which spread out into the square under rough shelters of all kinds of stalls. One can imagine the arguing and the shouting and the fights. Retribution was swift and easy: it was handy to administer punishment. Here the stocks were kept awaiting the felon to fill them and to give malicious pleasure to the crowds of spectators which where always available.

Only the faces of the crowds change as they watch the guests go in to the Hunt Balls or wait for the results of General Elections or buy and sell amongst the market stalls on the cobbled stones of Boscawen Square, in front of the Red Lion or between Waterloo House and John Cock the Brazier. Citizens dressed in their warmest clothes gathered to watch the horses and hounds on Boxing Day, to see them clatter over the smooth stones in a glorious pageant. After the wars other crowds moved in celebration to the old tune of the Floral Dance. My people have watched it all, been part of it. My father skated in the old rink and his same skates were used by my brother to spin down Lemon Street from top to bottom. The street was not the dizzy traffic scene of today lined with parked cars on both sides ... but it was just as steep and a dangerous achievement. Those heavy wheels rolling faster, gaining speed with every second. And if there were no cars there were horses and carts. There were the main shops where Mother bought her lengths of Tobralco or cotton: Roberts, Gills, and the West End. We never went into the smaller, exclusive shops. Mother made all our dresses. 'Aunty taught me,' she would say, and without a pattern or any guide she would run up dresses for Sylvia and myself. Uncle Robert, being an experienced tailor, made good coats for us: he was the professional. If we visited Aunt Delia's on a week night the round table would be covered with thick bales of cloth which were to be marked off with flat pieces of white chalk, strong, sure, white strokes ... ready for the scissors, cutting pieces of cloth to be stitched.

There was an iron and a cloth-covered ironing board in the kitchen which was soon to hiss with the steam of spit and it would be time for the artistry of shaping, the manipulating and the fitting of blue or brown suiting materials. Aunt Delia with pins held in her mouth would fix together the jig-saw pieces as she sat in her corner of the table. Granfer smoked his pipe in the armchair and all the while Raymond, our cousin who was like a brother, who cycled to fetch lemons or aspirin when we were ill and who laughed like a drain when he took me to the circus, practised on the piano. The incident which made him laugh so much was the clown raising his hand in order to deal a mighty blow to his partner and withdrawing all force at the moment of contact. I did this. Raymond was so amazed and laughed conspicuously. The clown played up when he saw the crowd was amused and repeated the gesture, each time with more success.

I said my father skated. He took advantage of every opportunity and somehow confounded all those of his generation who would in time compare their own youth with the years of indulgence and amenity granted to their sons or grandchildren.

Rarely did he confide but once he said to me, 'I was in the Boys' Brigade years ago. My friend who was a bugler had a cap. I didn't, so I bought one ready for the parade. I didn't know it was wrong. The Leader said, "My dear Willy, you can't go and promote yourself like that".'

He laughed when he told this story. I liked hearing it and then I thought it was out of character. Perhaps he realised this was one of life's hard lessons. He never deceived anyone, not that I knew of, and was truly respected by everyone: he had a reputation of being kind and straight, and naturally we thought of it as being well earned. He played always according to the rules.

My Father went into photography and by hiring himself out to take wedding pictures or family groups he earned enough to take him to evening classes where he studied accountancy. He joined the Male Voice Choir; he swam at Sunny Corner, Malpas, just opposite the sewage works. He said it was better in the dark - you thought the water was cleaner. He loved gymnastics, taking part in many competitions and displays.

Then World War 1 struck. This was a severe blow which was to ruin any ambition or plan he might have had. He joined the army and fought in France. Years later, after he died, many, many years later, I found a slip which he treasured. It said, 'A thoroughly reliable and trustworthy W.O. His service with this unit has been in every way satisfactory and I can recommend him to any who may require his services. Rule William James. Rank B Q M S. Regiment R.C.A.'

He did give his help to others unstintingly.

In one way he was successful: he made the most of his life all the time. He lived every moment. Afterwards I understood.

****** ****** ****** ****** ******

Communication Problems

His skin never browned in the sun even though quite a lot of his time was spent on the beach with the family he loved. I can see him now in my mind, sitting on the sand, looking a bit hard at something because he was temporarily without his glasses, drying his toes ... him with his white, city skin. And then, sitting in the bow of a rowing boat next to Uncle Joe who was brown like a walnut, he looked more townie than ever.

He loved the sea and swimming ... just as I did ... to be in it and part of it more than to be on it. At one time, when we were sitting on some rocks above a clear pool and were thinking of swimming, I saw his face, the infinite remembering and regret, and I thought, 'This is how I shall be one day.'

****** ****** ****** ****** ******

At that time I knew so little about him. Sometimes I longed to talk to him about things I considered important which happened at school and which I thought he would understand. But there was that barrier of reserve which kept secret all the thoughts and dreams he must have had. I wanted him to put his arms around me and he would have if I could have cuddled close to him, or climbed up on his knees as Sylvia did so easily. My own reserve made my approach more difficult.

On a summer's evening I can see him sitting under the trellis arch where our rambling roses grew. He would clean his nails and press down the cuticles on his fingers. He always thought this important. Most of the time he would be watching us play on the lawn, tumbling or doing cartwheels; if Howard was there we might be playing badminton over the rope he had tied across the middle of the lawn. He was relaxed, his grey eyes filled with pride and love. He would quote from 'The Village Blacksmith'; I think this was the only poem he knew. He never was one for reading books ... newspapers and his 'Taxation', the periodical which kept him up to date with his work, were his limit. I think he despised, maybe, a little, what was deemed useless knowledge. Though he made time for pleasure, ours as well as his own.

However I could get through to Mother in spite of her not being given to expansive gestures of affection. She would tuck us up in bed, shout at times and give the odd slap which we ignored or dodged. Like herd animals who acknowledge the pack leader we wanted no discipline from other sources. Later I knew too well how much we had all taken her for granted. Then I grieved over the personality which never emerged. The stubborn woman, loyal, frustrated at times, but always responding to

CARLYN.

the light. Her success, she maintained, was in the existence of her three children who were healthy, very happy and reasonably successful. Discerning, fey and underestimated, Mother was the only one in those years to tell me I had the makings of an eccentric woman, and I laughed as I held up my Father's umbrella which I had borrowed in case it rained at the carnival. She made certain that always there was a sense of security and togetherness which lasted up until the day that Father died.

Carlyn, our new house, was the beginning and the end of our move away from the integral folk origins, and Mother was more conscious of the break than anyone. The house was built near the top of Daniell Road. From the back it looked over a field and the trees which lined Redannick Lane and the cluster of houses which ringed the dominating Cathedral. At one time there was a castle to the left where the market was and my father had been born in its precincts; this must have been the commercial and political centre ... St Mary's Church before the Cathedral, the religious focus. Moresk and Castle Hill, Pydar Street and River Street, Kenwyn Street and Calenick Street led from the Market Square to the County areas beyond the town, Redruth and Camborne, St Austell and St Agnes, a few of the places where beacons flared out on historic occasions and flared with more sinister motives in our pagan times.

****** ****** ****** ****** ******

On Saturday nights Truro streets teemed with people and vendors still traded from open stalls on market days. Because we lived in Carlyn at the top of Daniell Road we were distanced from the heart of all this and yet not far enough to be absorbed into the established Middle Classes, who lived at the top of Lemon Street or Strangways Terrace or in the Georgian houses in River Street.

Yes, we were distanced from the heart of the town and the old characters like Minnie Googe, Bessie Webber, Freddie Snell who once was brought in to a Christmas Dinner at Aunt Delia's. And we lost contact with the neighbours in Fairmantle Street, especially a coloured family, Mrs Cockle and her five sons who were friends of Howard. Mr Cockle was a seaman and was away most of the time on his ship and the boys, Harrison, John, William, Victor, George and Emmanuel, were accepted without question in the city of Truro.

Mrs Cockle, Mother said, was a lady.

If they knew just how much their memory lingered in my mother's so many years later! How they came in one Christmas when we lived in Fairmantle Street to listen to *Messiah*, being played on an old gramophone with a trumpet in the front room. And how, during her last months,

Mother would say, 'Now then, let me run through the boys, the Cockles again. Let me see, Harrison, Willy, Victor, George and Emmanuel.'

After this she would smile with satisfaction. 'I can see them now.'

Fairmantle Street is a faint memory.

On the mahogany chest of drawers there is a faded scorch mark. It is disappointing to think I cannot remember my most dramatic moment and can only report hearsay.

Howard was left in charge of me when I was about three years old and the candle on the chest of drawers burnt down so that the wood began to smoulder.

Mother said, 'When I came in the room was blue with smoke. I couldn't see the bed, let alone you. Well, I shouted for Will, struggled over and picked you up. You were a dead weight. "Will," I said, "she's gone." Will opened the window and all the other windows in the house and ... '

'Then you boxed my ears,' Howard would add if he were there.

'Did you call the fire brigade?' When I first heard the story I revelled in my first starring role. I saw a fragile child in her mother's arms and heard the clanging of the fire engine bell. Just like a page of Mother's book.

'No. We rolled up the cloth, dipped it in the big jug on the wash-stand and that was that.'

No real memories of life in Fairmantle Street, only scrappy thoughts.

There was an organ in the kitchen and a glass window over the passage door. The kitchen door opened into a cupboard of a back kitchen where there was a tap and a bucket into which Howard pretended to be sick when it was time for Sunday School. The back kitchen opened into a yard which was shared by all the people in the neighbouring houses ... Fairmantle Street and Tabernacle Street. In this yard daytime rows and moonlit gossip prevailed.

We had a black spaniel dog called Toby who played quite a part in our home life and perhaps more in the walks and scrapes of Howard, Raymond and Frank. He was intelligent; 'sly', Mother called him. If we were in bed and Mother left the house he would wait until the door clicked behind her and then would run upstairs to nuzzle his way into the warmth of our blankets. If he became too muddy and disreputable in his wanderings around Truro he did not dare return to our house but he scraped at Aunt Delia's door to be tidied up and returned with her apologies. Whilst on holiday at St Agnes when he swam in the green waves under the cliffs visitors sometimes thought he was a seal and his black head sliding under green waves made a good holiday snap.

We spent our Saturday's penny in the corner shop owned by Mrs Grant with her dark bobbed hair and gentle smile. She measured out our triangular packets of jelly babies or liquorice or stripy peppermints. If we were careful with our spending we had a halfpenny change.

There was a pump at the end of the street.

There were few cars at the time, so I ask, 'How did we move so freely between the homes of our aunts?' The one car journey I remember was in a vintage type owned by Chester from St Mawes who ran a taxi service in between his other brilliant enterprises. Three of us with the suit-cases were packed into the sprung-up, blown-back discomfort of the Dickey-seat. Others travelled inside as in a stage coach. We went via Tregony, the long journey to St Mawes.

Most times we used our water-way, the River Fal. During holidays, Saturdays, probably Sundays (although Chapel and Sunday School were important in our family), maybe two boats would be hired at Malpas and the combined families of Mother and Aunt Delia and Frank, who stayed with us often, piled in with baskets and bathing costumes, tea cloths and towels and made our way down the Fal.

The splash of oars, the laughing, the boys singing 'Bill Smith loves our Fa-a-ather, Father loves Bill Smith' over and over. Aunt Delia and Mother wearing bright scarves, the men in panama hats and the boys stripped to the waist.

If we went to St Anthony, Uncle Robert organised a cricket match which we played on the grassland below the lighthouse. 'We'll put the girls in first, get them out, then we can play all afternoon.' Our captain with his one leg was in command.

We never thought of leaving until dusk and often there was a long row back across a river flooded by moonlight.

****** ****** ****** ****** ******

Behind the Cathedral the rim of town houses was contained in a ring of green fields. To the left the line of houses in Hendra made their light patterns at night, and directly in front, on our horizon, were the spoil tips from the St Austell China Clay Works, not distant yet as important as the remote sphinx.

Returning from a visit to Falmouth where I had been sent, I suppose, to be out of the way during the removal, I entered with Sylvia the hollow, new-wood-smelling, high-ceilinged house. I was quiet but sensed that this was something which Mother and Father wanted to show us, and was important. Dad said, 'See this switch on the wall?'

I looked at a brown, round fixture on the cold wall which had a small lever in front.

'Now then, press that down.'

I pressed and the light flared in the room. I looked around. So this was the reason for their pride. At Carlyn there was to be no lighting up at dusk; no careful cosseting of gas mantles or rose-coloured glass shades which warmed the night.

Carlyn was cold. Four winds took it in turns to buffet its walls. Rain beat on the square windows and in time seeped into the house. It was a house which never became cosy in spite of a Cornish Range in the kitchen which heated the room and water as well as cooking our food. On Sundays there was a banked fire in one of the sitting rooms which was glowing red to look at yet was wasted. We never seemed to be the kind of family to gather round a fire ... except at Christmas.

All intimate conversations took place around the kitchen table, which was usually covered with a chequered cloth. Above us, in his own palace of a cage, swung Beauty, the Budgie. He might have been pale blue or green, he might even have been a she, but Beauty was always listening. These conversations were frank, and strangely, for our family, quite intimate. There was a diffidence which was ingrained in all of us. None of us ever really conquered this defect. It was very rare for us to consider the world outside our own family and parochial affairs, partly because we never ventured into such a different territory. I suppose we might be considered a complete unit. Sometimes, however, a hint of how dangerous the outside world could be was conveyed.

The conspiratorial atmosphere was established. There was the lazy putting-off clearing of dishes and debris of our meal, and a pushing-away of plates to the centre of the table so that our elbows could rest more easily.

Father moved from his seat, went to the back kitchen and washed his hands, put on his coat and trilby hat, said, 'Well, I'll be off now,' and returned to his office. Six times a day he walked the length of Daniell Street, Lemon Street and across the town. He walked with an even, bouncy step and was able to maintain this habit even when most men of his age had lost their own youthful vitality.

As soon as the door closed behind him and we had heard the sound of the gate, our meeting began. The teapot was cold under the cosy ... there were no drinks, no lighting of cigarettes, just the room for our elbows. Howard, Sylvia and I shuffled our chairs a bit so that we used up the extra room. Maybe there were small items of news, little things which happened at school perhaps.

For a wonder, at these times, Mother was the listener. She had a limited social life, her main outing being the Wednesday shopping trip. She was content with the regular round to Brewer's and Lipton's for flour, butter, biscuits - always biscuits: coconut macaroons and her thin wafers, the plain family biscuits for us and gingerbreads which were Father's favourites. The routine was as regular as the teatime meal of brawn and pickles we had on Wednesdays. There were no supermarkets in those days. The housewives did not have afternoon teas either: friends met and gossiped in King Street or Boscawen Street. Plenty of acquaintances, for Wednesday was Market Day. From the top of Castle Hill the lowing of cattle could be heard and the burr in the voices around was more pronounced.

However, around the table Mother listened. She had heard all the office news during the meal; now it was our turn. The conversations became longer and much more interesting when Howard was out of his early teenage and was in his last years at school. A gentleman in the area had invited him to go on a trip to London as a companion. Such a significant event it seems now, and fraught with all kinds of connotations, but all was innocent. Absolute honesty around that table made this fact clear, yet now we heard that it was possible for a youth to be an object of attraction, and not only for the opposite sex. In all this Mother was as avid for information as ourselves: her searching questions and Howard's answers - not embellished to any great degree - provided us with at least a basic knowledge.

In the cold back kitchen where the winds of the North and East forced under the door and through the eaves we would wait for Father to come home from work. Mother would begin a peculiar rhythmic stamping.

A Lumpy-dump,
A Lumpy-dump,
Dumpety-dump,
Dumpety-dump.

Imitating, we would fold our arms and join her. The wooden floor over the cellar beneath echoed and made more mysterious the beat:

A Lumpy-dump.

We never managed to simulate the stance. The square, hunched, dumpy outline of a human determined to defeat any discomfort or evil was on its own. I realised this was when I first noticed her special way of self-protection. An unkind word, a threat, a displeasing thought and the shoulders would square, the head would recede a little and the whole body would bunch. Then anyone who would dare might attack. So bucolic a memory, I am almost ashamed to record it, yet it remains an essential fragment of our family life.

I wondered why we did not just stay in the kitchen in the warm.

****** ****** ****** ****** ******

Family Rows

These blew up without reason as is usual in most families.

Three of us would be sitting round the Cornish Range as we waited for Father and Howard to return. Mother and I would argue. I could always argue with Mother. She said things all the time that no one could ever agree with and Mother was not at the top of the 'pecking order.' Not one of us would dare answer Father back so he never argued.

Then Sylvia, dulcet sweet, would begin her soothing act. In a moment the nature of the row changed. The cheerful wrangle became a storm of words, there would be real anger, shouting and suddenly Mother and I would be on the same side and Sylvia in tears ... words. The house, although it was grey, square, cold and gravelly, became our home. There was plenty of light and swirls of air. I recall my last night spent in the house when the curtains had been stripped, ready for removal; a night I shall remember always. So empty, moonlight flooding through the windows. I lay awake just to absorb every detail of the about-to-be-lost whispering atmosphere. I wanted to be able to report with accuracy back to my Mother who was going to spend the rest of her widowed years with my husband and myself. The austerity, the deserted rooms, stripped furniture save for my makeshift bed; the brilliant, silver-blue light flaring through the leaves of our laburnum and cherry trees outside to enter the bedroom where my Mother and Father had spent most of their long married life.

The spirit of my father remained. Austere, remote, conscientious, assiduous, 'thoroughly reliable and trustworthy' said the army reference. But there was ambition which was like steel, smooth forged, without the cutting edge of ruthlessness. There was loyalty and warmth and a latent need for appreciation which was, I think, denied him in our young heedless years. We admired him too much and placed him too high in our esteem ... We were a little in awe. Yet this was simply lack of communication and the generation gap.

****** ****** ****** ****** ******

Family Gatherings

There were frequent gatherings in the favourite family houses. The sisters exchanged gossip. Neighbours called on these occasions. A conversational theme was discovered, the vein tapped and traced through all the episodes and explanations and plans. In all of us, the women - well, females, for we were young then - there was a fascination in the supernatural ... a sensitivity, awareness of vibrations, whatever. We were fey. Aunt Gertie told fortunes and made some extra 'silver' by telling fortunes to the wealthy summer visitors. She gained quite a reputation until, quite suddenly, 'She lost it,' so she said.

Aunt Flo with her tea-leaves and cards was uncanny. Even in her last years, friends begged her, 'Let's have a look in my cup, Flo.' Later Mother joined the coven and bought a crystal. The very fact of buying this was fraught with laughter. She made a name for herself in the local fetes and money-raising efforts for the community. This was where any imagination we had was fostered, and why our school friends never knew what to make of us.

****** ****** ****** ****** ******

A Trip to Plymouth

Plymouth Argyle was playing at home. This meant a family outing, a train journey to Plymouth. It meant shopping for us and the excitement of the football match for Father and Howard.

The train journey was exciting enough and Plymouth was the nearest big town for the people in Cornwall. Crowds poured from the station and streamed into the streets where shops displayed all kinds of goods which had not so far been shown in the country markets of the west. If there was a wedding or if anything special at all was required, that item would be bought on one of these expeditions.

Spooners, the Mecca, was a department store so large that we dared not let each other out of sight. The white starched tablecloths in the restaurant showed up bright cutlery and we sat, smelling the kitchen smells of roast potatoes, fried fish and steaming cabbage. Waitresses were young beautiful girls who seemed to us like film stars. They brought out our chosen dishes and we forgot our awe in our need to satisfy young and inquisitive hunger. After lunch Father and Howard caught the bus to the football ground and Sylvia, Mother and I trailed with anticipation around the stores. Probably a new handbag, a hat, a costume or coat for Mother would be inside the paper carriers marked 'Spooners'. Whatever happened, shopping was intended to last the whole of the afternoon.

Howard and Dad appeared at teatime. They would be mingling in the expanding crowd. Maybe Father would spot us first. He would see Mother's hat, as familiar as an old pair of slippers. He would whistle the family signal and we would all meet. If Mother spotted him first she would cry, her west-country voice more noticeable in the town store, 'Over 'ere, Will.'

It was always a family occasion and we remained together, travelling by tram to the Palace Theatre where we saw in real life some of the well-known stars of the day ... Kitty Masters and Ella Shields amongst others. I think it was the tram journey I remember most, the sliding, slippery regular beat and the smoothness of the lighted cabs as they hummed through the street. Before going to the station for our train we called at a fish and chip shop opposite the theatre.

Yes, the packet with our piece of fish, chips and - a touch which always reminds me of Plymouth - a little lump moulded from sweet, mushy peas. There would be another bus to carry us to the station, then a moment of confusion, sounds of shunting trains and shouts and a sight of a lot of legs and the entry into the carriage which was to take us home.

To Sylvia and myself, the hissing steam and whistles, the moving crowds, became a background which grew less noisy all the time until it faded absolutely. Perhaps the last memory might be the rough upholstery and the sepia pictures above each seat. Neither of us will ever be definite.

I can recall after this, only the 'tired and teasy' accusations from Mother before the delicious moment when our bodies were curled under the top clothes of our own bed.

CHAPTER 6

School Memories and School Friends

I watched the High School girls walk along Treyew Road which led between their school, a gracious building set amongst trees and silence in Falmouth Road, and Dalvenie, the brown, sandstone house where the boarders lived. Dalvenie was opposite our County School. This was long and looked new and I suppose was adequate for the girls who with no social aspirations were anxious to learn so that they might have just enough knowledge to hold their own in a world which was now changing. The High School girls had brown gym slips which were fashioned in a way to make their bodies look slim and elegant, and they wore pink blouses, which unfairly flattered them, or so it appeared to us.

Their features also were enhanced by the real Panama hats they wore in summer. In winter, tailored coats and hats in brown looked just as well. Our school uniform was ugly, black gym slips with white blouses and red girdles. The horrible square hats which we crammed down over our heads were something to remember.

Their voices were muted and pleasant; they did not play around or laugh or do anything to break the pattern of their group. If they did notice us they suppressed all sign of it in their whole demeanour. We said they were snobs. My father would have appreciated their effortless formation, a tidy, gently weaving crocodile. He liked parades. In fact he enjoyed the discipline, the trappings and toggery of any society to which he belonged. Not to the extreme: our family would have mocked even him out of any hint of ostentatiousness. I was the opposite, then, always on the edge, and although I was included and enjoyed the small happenings around me, I was most happy on my own ... as long as there were people, I say paradoxically ... To be free to come and go. I hated uniform mostly because I looked awful in uniform and if I had known I would spend all my working years in uniform I would have been defeated at the beginning.

No wonder I sought so many means of escape.

But Father was in the Oddfellows, the Freemasons, the reserves of the R.G.A., the Choir. He liked his club ... but he did try to wear his cap in the Boys' Brigade before he earned it.

In spite of all this I did envy the High School girls.

The walls were so new inside our school; granite as strong and as clean as any stone in the world could be; wide windows and empty corridors which, at regular intervals, swished with the sound of our footsteps and rustle of the serge gym slips. The 'mistresses', we called them, were older than contemporary teachers (or this may be a sign of my own age: as the years progress, policemen become almost infants). I recognised each voice if they conversed with each other outside the classroom; I knew, as if I had helped them choose, their collection of clothes, the way folds of material fell in their skirts, their favourite colours and, of course, we all knew where they lodged in the road which led to the school.

These houses were run by genteel ladies; probably most of these were widowed. We were familiar with the comings and goings of different members of the staff. None of our female teachers was married (a career woman was a career woman in those days), and we knew who was friendly with whom. We knew how some had become intimate friends and no suspicions of unhealthy associations ever entered our innocent minds. Oh ... we were well-behaved ... how quietly we walked on the beige floors or those airy corridors in our gym shoes and black pleated tunics! How we appreciated those occasions when as a treat we were allowed to weed Miss Foreman's garden! Miss Foreman was the Head Mistress. However, we never managed to arouse enthusiasm for those enforced sessions of digging out plantains from the hockey field at all.

Miss Foreman was in her late thirties perhaps, as we judged. I remember her wearing soft brown tweeds. She was not over large, yet the sight of her would command respect and interest. She took English classes.

She entered the classroom and stood on the small dais in front of the cleaned blackboard. Once it was covered with curly brackets, my particular doodle. She asked who was responsible. I did not answer, not because I was afraid of punishment, nor because I wanted to blame anyone else, but because I had been squiggling with chalk without realising. She looked at me, quite long and hard; I said nothing. She too said nothing, only asked me to clean the board with a rubber which has not changed in design much over the years. It was afterwards, when it was too late, that I knew it was myself and now the feeling of guilt still sweeps over me as I remember. How sly and cowardly she must have considered me! Yet her kind attitude had nothing of the patronising and forgiving saint about it. I think she understood, better than my friends in the classroom who had railed and ranted about the incident later.

She made no secret that I was her favourite. I can see her chalked question being squeaked on the blackboard, I remember the way she would turn to face the class and the way her brown eyes would search for mine. The way she found them, finally, for my head would be lowered as I tried to concentrate on the books or papers in front of me. 'Now Marjory,' she would say, 'tell us ... in your own words ... What do you think?' And I hated myself because I did know the answer.

I never thought of myself as an achiever in those laid-back years, although I enjoyed most of my lessons and revelled in the outdoor games. In everything I was average and caused surprise only once in my school assessment time when I found that with two girls who were known to be brilliant I had also a mark of over seventy-five percent in all my subjects. But I think I had an edge on them because I was included in the sports scene at school, which they were not. If I did achieve a record it was when I had most Order Marks for bad conduct and the most 'Excellents' for good work at the same time. We had different standards, remember, and one had only to be noisy or laugh or be late to be reprimanded. Vandalism was unheard of in those days.

Miss Foreman singled me out sometimes for praise and I cringed. English was my favourite lesson. I discovered I could follow her thoughts with ease and wanted, with an urgency I had never experienced previously, to utter my own thoughts aloud. I wanted to join in her flights of imagination, enter the bright world she was explaining. Now, I know how much she encouraged me and that she was trying to make me speak and when she said, 'What do you think about this?' or 'Tell me your idea,' she meant to encourage me. But she tried too hard. If I answered, her response would be effusive, she would praise too highly so that I would retreat into myself, wishing I had never spoken. Only in the back rows of the unawakened children did I feel secure. She said once I was the absolute example of the all-rounder, meaning to praise me, but this flung me into a familiar state of confusion.

School days passed in a haze of summer, bees droned in the hedges and there were long, lazy walks through grass grown high enough to be tipped with rosy hay seeds.

There were busy learning days, and evenings when homework was skipped in order to spend time with friends who had tennis courts and parents who treated their children and their friends as young adults. This was not a familiar experience to me. Several times I was invited to stay with a school friend, so different from a visit to one of my aunts.

It was exciting to go into the car with Beryl on the first visit to her home. Her parents travelled miles each day to take her from her home in Gerrans and back from school. She was a quiet girl, efficient and practical in her school work, and spoke more easily to me than to the others. I thought she was attractive. Beryl had brown eyes and long blond hair which she plaited. I suppose our friendship began when I met her during my stays at St Mawes. I would walk to St Just Headland and whistle for the ferry man whose row-boat would then be certain to creak easily across the water to pick me up. Beryl waited on the other side, skimming flat stones across the dark water to pass the time; it was never more than about a quarter of an hour. We would then walk to her home, maybe, for lunch, or begin our afternoon by going down the hill to Portscatho and along the cliff path. The beaten path, where once they burnt furze bushes to attract wrecks, was gold with wheat on one side and deep, deep blue on the other. This was where my Grandfather was shipwrecked. I would tell Beryl my bit of family history and she would laugh.

Staying in her house, however, was very different. Her father was a schoolmaster and her mother was a dark, older version of Beryl. I could not speak to them easily at first, but watched with fascination at the way Beryl behaved on quite equal terms with her parents. She did help me to feel at ease with a kind of indulgent politeness. The formal breakfast was for me a revelation: it was the first, typical English, middle-class breakfast I ever had. This must seem an amazing fact coming from a successful accountant's daughter. I came down the carpeted cosy stairs of this country cottage whose windows overlooked a narrow road and the churchyard. When I came downstairs on those mornings, I smelled bacon frying and toast, a lovely breakfast smell, but was a little puzzled by a quick flurry of organised activity from Beryl's mother. She had already made a start on the housework. I could hear her moving upstairs as she finished her bedmaking and dusting. Such organisation! She was down before we had seated ourselves around the table. Afterwards not a moment of precious time was to be wasted. We gardened like a troop of soldiers on routine duties. Beryl took me to the flower borders to weed while her mother saw to the roses before taking the mowing machine around the lawn; her father tended the vegetable plot and saw to the tennis court. Afterwards I helped Beryl in her grandmother's general village shop. This was when I saw my friend in a different light. She brought out, with efficiency, bottles of Corona in wooden crates and with expertise she sorted tins of corned beef and boxes of Blue Cross Matches, packets of Reckitt's Blue, placing them on the shelves within easy reach of her grandmother and herself. Then she prepared the 'orders'. I felt useless. Yet Beryl's grandmother seemed nearer to the people I knew. Her sharp tongue which controlled her customers and the interest she displayed as she questioned each one with natural curiosity, reminded me of my aunts. In the evening there was tennis and this was my first taste of the regulated, simple, middle-class way of life. It was strange ... well ... so organised.

A similar experience was to stay with Gillian who lived in the same village. Her parents kept a guest house in Gerrans. Here also there was a close relationship in the family but I was aware of a more intellectual atmosphere. They read books, were interested in music and took time to watch the beauty around them. One thing that impressed me which explains, perhaps, more about my own family, was the affectionate relationship between the three of them.

Just before bedtime Gillian's father stood behind Gillian's chair and began brushing her long, black hair which, in school, she wore in tight pigtails. Gillian accepted this attention with a shrug of her shoulders and smiled her tip-tilted smile at me. I did smile back but lowered my eyes towards the basket of foliage which was placed in the grate. Conversation continued between them all the while, for they saw nothing remarkable in the situation at all. It was natural for them to touch each other, show all the affection they felt and talk. Gillian's parents were both young and attractive. They took us to St Mawes for the evening and we spent the evening at the Idle Rocks. Me ... in the

Idle Rocks! It might have been a palace to us and not even Uncle Joe would dream of taking a drink in this bar. The family probably knew of my own connections with St Mawes because I had often spoken of them to Gillian but they never mentioned them.

I liked both Gillian and Beryl very much, though I was never with both of them together. This happens often: different people match different facets in the personality.

In Truro there were other friends. One who called for me each day to go to school was Pauline. She would come in and sit on a little seat outside our front door. She said our family laughed more than anyone else she knew. Pauline and I would go on our way and like migrating swallows gathered numbers on the road. I met Joy, who came from Old Falmouth Road, up by the seats at the top of Daniell Road. We knew each front garden and the shape of every house along our school road but we never saw the inhabitants. One garden had a bay tree and when mother had herrings to marinade we were told to bring back some of the leaves.

Enthusiasm for a meal of marinaded herrings was predictable after a visit, quite rare in those days, to St. Ives. An evening stroll through those twisting street lanes meant one was exposed to the exquisite fragrance, to a Cornishman at any rate, of slow-cooking herrings in night ovens. Fresh herrings would be laid in a clome dish, covered with vinegar and water, seasoned and made aromatic by the addition of a few bay leaves. Each member of our family found the smell irresistible but frustrating. This was not a dish that one could find in a restaurant or buy in a fish and chip shop. This was a native delicacy and was strictly for the genuine locals who kept up their own traditions. This was one of the times when my father seemed funny and vulnerable. Like a Bisto Kid, his face lifted into the air the better to enjoy the smells, and I swear his mouth watered.

Truro friends came on winter walks with me. We walked round Penwhithers, over the moors at Baldhu. Baldhu leading from Penwhithers was a walk mostly taken by Sylvia and me. In sunlight or moonlight we trudged across the heather. On summer evenings we saw red and gold sunset skies, and in those safe pre-war days we walked in the magic of moonlit evenings. We went to Calenick to catch tadpoles: Calenick was my destination whenever I decided to run away from home. Why I chose this spot I never understood, yet this was where I headed and this was where I was certain that one member of the family would find me. Calenick was a sleepy hamlet, wooded and green and crusted with white thatched cottages. The cottages were bordered by patchwork gardens with wide, rounded walls. These we passed on the way to a muddy splat when the tide was low to collect our tadpoles. And why did we want them? Calenick used to be on the old Falmouth road and probably had much more importance before the time of our own youth. It was a meandering old coach road and was used long before traffic streamed along the modern road. Yet this area is sufficiently rural still to satisfy hordes of summer visitors. The Old Coach Road, however, was familiar only to the locals. Our lives were spent going to all the places around us, seeing so many important things and having so much to talk about all the time.

****** ****** ****** ****** ******

Wheels Made a Difference

Two shops made an impact on the lives of my sister and myself. On Saturday nights when a great deal of the shopping was done (shops stayed open until all hours then) we had our treat. Father took Mother and Sylvia and me to Davey's the Fruiterers in the High Street. Upstairs in a clean, fresh-smelling room we sat at a table by the window which looked out on King Street and enjoyed an ice-cream. This was no ordinary ice-cream but an ice-cream made deliciously from a closely guarded secret family recipe. It was topped with a spoonful of Cornish Cream. The vanilla smell and the cool freshness of that room on a sultry summer evening is a unique memory.

The other shop had such a contrasting smell. It smelt of engine oil and rubber and gleamed with the hard brightness of steel. This was where our parents took Sylvia and me on the evening they bought us our bicycles. There was a sound too, sensuous and exciting, the gritty, grasping, efficient smoothness as the pedal manoeuvred the wheel. Mr Langdon lifted the bicycles off the ground to demonstrate, his brown face triumphant. 'You can tell, Bill,' he said. 'You can tell.' I cannot describe the joy, only know that on those wheels life became wider and more free.

Now summer evenings meant cycle rides between high Cornish hedges along lanes that later were expected to take noisy streams of holiday traffic. Glimpse of blue sea through foxgloves promised fresh salt winds and an evening swim. We knew where the Atlantic and the English Channel were, even without seeing the water, because above would be an extra clarity of sky and a windy emptiness.

In our home our meal table was set for five places. This was how it had been, and at that time I thought this was as it always would be as long as I said my prayers with conviction every night. Please God do not let Mummy or Daddy, Howard or Sylvia or any other person in our family die, be killed, burned or drowned this year or the next year for ever and ever. Amen.

The first threat to this familiar warmth came on the night Sylvia was rushed home from a Girl Guide camp at Manaccan with an inflamed appendix. Here I must mention that this was a much more serious illness in those days before penicillin prevented such drastic after effects. Sylvia and her friends had eaten a lot of green apples, which had aggravated the symptoms and made the condition dangerous enough for me to imagine what life would be like without the round, lovable, brown-eyed companion that I took so much for granted. Her place at the table for those weeks whilst she was in hospital was like an empty shrine. But she recovered.

Now it was my turn to take advantage of the fact that we were always to be treated alike. I was to stay with Sylvia during her convalescence at Perranporth.

There was a house which was perched on the cliff on the way up to Droskyn Point. Mrs Kellow and her daughter kept this as a boarding house. They were clients of my father and this was where we were to stay. From the window we could see the long stretch of sand sifting and changing from white to gold, lifting and stinging across the beach, sometimes covering, as it did once upon a time, as much as a whole village. There was the Lost Church at Perranzabuloe and the narrow lanes which led from the beach to secret houses and inns, roads used for carrying forbidden goods for those who could pay. There were, then, rivers running red with raddled ore over the beach at St Agnes and there were the rocks with names, Chapel Rock, the Cow and Calf and others. The sea town was different from others we knew. It was much more open, Atlantic waves spreading white all the length of the shore; waves which turned on themselves to break into foamy showers or to flow with force on to the sand. More open, and yet the land behind was wild and secret. Chapel Rock might have been the site for some ancient form of worship - maybe it was connected with a burial ground - but there is an aura about it which has not dimmed in spite of all the cups of tea drunk or pasties eaten by generations on its smooth stones. It is said that a hermit's chapel stood on it in the Middle Ages.

Outside the house the road was nothing more than a path to the cliffs. I could walk to the edge of the sea at high tide and see each wave come in separately. Dark green, almost black but always sinister, with a warning of power.

Mrs Kellow and her daughter enjoyed having us. They shared a gift of being able to tell by looking at a person what their birth sign was. They were always right. It was a novel experience for me to go to school by travelling on the local train and to meet groups of children from different schools. And to return to the house at night where there was a smell, autumnal and spicy, of baked apples. The air was chilled with Atlantic winds and tasted of washed salt. It was extra exhilarating because it was a new sensation of freedom and I was to enjoy it without having to suffer an appendix operation. It was the first time we had been linked together as somebody else's children. Just two little girls, I suppose, spoilt by all those aunts who had sons, and so secure in our family bonds. But it would be a long time before we would have our own identity.

I was the one in the middle, neither fish nor fowl nor good red herring; not the first born, old enough to have friends, school subjects important to study in seclusion and a life of his own, and yet not young enough to be the family pet. I was the one whose fate seems to be to withdraw and to watch with envy. Sylvia would catch hold of Howard's hand or climb on to Father's knee. When I was to go to the County School it meant that we both went; when there was a new dress or a new coat to be fitted, we both had the same, and we were not even twins.

If I could have only explained this ... but there was no one to understand.

So often I have asked, 'Where do I stand? What is it that makes me?' or 'Who am I?'

Far off in time and place Percy was a hindsman. Great-grandfather was a sea captain; mother's people were smugglers and seamen and miners at Hugus. Grandfather's mother Cordelia was a 'lady' and her brother, seaman as he was, lived a life of freedom and had some standing. Father's people were Methodist ministers. His mother was used to genteel people around her for when she was young she worked as lady's companion in a big house; it is true to say there were some landed people amongst both sides. Aunt Flo could tell stories; Father was ambitious and gregarious and Mother was stubborn and loyal and capable of being a really good business woman.

They came from the sea and the land, and beneath the land some of them worked, and I am made up of fragments. If a dog comes to me and I stroke it, if I have an empathy with a horse or an affinity with any animal, then I am the hindsman. When I run into the sea as if it will wrap round me and support me and I feel the exhilaration of the stinging cold, I am the sailor. When I sense the mystery of the earth and the songs in all the trees and yearn into the mists of the night I am the child of nature, and when I want to sing of the wonders I see or laugh at the life around me, I am Aunty Flo.

CHAPTER SEVEN

A Walk by the Fal

To cross the River Fal at St Michael Penkivel, or at Tolverne or King Harry or on the stout steam ferries across from Falmouth to St Mawes or Trefusis was a water journey to be enjoyed. At the time, although I had never heard of the word 'sensual', this was more than a pleasing Saturday afternoon walk. I was not conscious of the freedom of movement, or any separate pleasure; the smells: malty smells as we walked past the warehouses, river smells as we walked along the head of the River Fal, the smell of vegetation as we passed between the two parts of Boscawen Park. In the first was the mysterious collection of shrubs and trees with the swans decorating its small lake ... and opposite, there was the open area which bordered the Fal where we played tennis and the boys played cricket in later years. I absorbed into my whole being sounds of the gulls, some shouts of the men on the beach at Malpas, a rhythmic, wooden sound of oars in the rowlocks and sights which I saw and took so much for granted. I saw the changing reflections on the river, the thick, wooded edge of the inlet at Tolverne, the tiny corner of cottages which made up the hamlet of St Clement. My father, Sylvia and I walked at a reasonable pace on the streets, through the paths and the trees, along the road around Tresillian, and took in, as our right, the beauty and life. Only in later years did I realise how much of it was instilled in my mind. The dark blue or grey silver waters shone with reflections of small craft or made a setting for rusted ocean-going ships which were laid up for resting periods. So many occasions which were important in our lives had the picture setting of the tree-lined river. Not only in our lives. Tristan and Isolde escaped across from Malpas to St Michael Penkivel, and the chapel dedicated to King Henry VI and Our Lady on the Tolverne side led to the ferry at Kebellans becoming famous ... the King Harry Ferry, which later was to become important to all our family, mainly through my Father's business interests. At Restronguet near Feock and at Mylor were little landing beaches for an ancient ferry. All these ferries had associations with our childhood; gave me those memories of dry, cold winter afternoons. The walk which began on the narrow, winter-foliaged lane to Malpas itself ... Mopas, we called it

MALPAS : THE SITE OF THE FERRY

then. 'Down Mopas' was the name for this mysterious annex for our childhood in Truro.

At Malpas we shouted across to where 'The Ship' used to be, for the ferryman to come over. If our shouts failed to attract his attention, the old deaf woman who lived under an upturned boat would add her own shrill scream, always effective. Across the cold water and then a walk through rustling, brown leaves where I would leap and skip high enough to reach the empty branches of the trees, running ahead of my father and Sylvia. The little patches of water seemed like frozen chips of winter magic. Then a more formal walk past the woods at Trewarthenick until we reached the main road from Bodmin which would lead us back to the quay at the bottom of Lemon Street and the tired drag up Daniell Road to our home, Carlyn. On a day like this Mother made hot potato cake which tasted more delicious because of our ravenous appetites.

Two pounds of mashed potatoes, eight ounces of suet, bind with an egg and bake in a hot oven to brown.

This was the walk! And on a day like this the family warmth was generated. The world was perfect and the relationships between members of our family were perfect.

I have mentioned Baldhu and a walk around to the Old Kea Board School which was always enjoyed, but there was also another factor, mystical, which I did not connect then to the spirit of the past. My great-grandmother and great-grandfather were married in Baldhu; their people had walked these places long years before, seen the same sun set. My Mother has told me stories about her relations who lived around this area so many times. How Percy, her cousin, had to go to Devoran to fetch the doctor when his mother, her Aunt Evelyn, was ill. What a terrible night it was, and how the Doctor picked up Percy in his trap on his way back to the call out. How Aunt Evelyn died and then her husband and the two young boys were sent by the Estate owner out to America to work on a ranch, more or less as slaves. One grew up and had enough guts to buy his way out and eventually to own his own ranch and his daughter came back to stay at our home years later, her object to find her mother's grave in Kea churchyard. These whispers from the past did come through to me, I am certain. Places have an atmosphere that is made up of people and incidents which they hold within them, maybe to divulge a little of their secret to those who will listen, so that they will live themselves ... and they do ... I have heard them breathe.

But the bicycles changed things a lot and I think these were the last of my special walks. Wheels which flew on weekends and evenings to less familiar places. I began to know the sensation of wind and the spray of the Atlantic and to experience the thrill of surfing on our fierce white breakers.

A Walk by the Fal

The world was widening. Even our holidays were in different places like Hayle Towans, where we rented a hut. This was a new kind of place, small undulating mounds with huts, all shapes and sizes and in all colours, and morning walks to the edge of the sea before returning in a concerted smell of bacon and eggs frying in the exhilarating air. Howard and Frank stayed with us at times, or Sylvia's friend, Peggy, who was getting thinner and more frail each year. Consumption was incurable at that time. My father joined us when he had his own holiday, or else he travelled to and from Truro. In the last years when the important school examinations were over, life seemed to stretch before us. The nights were often better than the days. Cool when the sun was too warm and starlight which was made dim by the brilliance of lights from across the water at St Ives. Lights and their reflections sending out sparks of emotion, making us feel the wonder was all too much and could never last.

Each big town had its holiday place. As in a summer resort for residents these places were where they relaxed. At Truro it was Perranporth. We went there often during the last of our school years. The beach at Perranporth stretched towards a range of sand mountains. White as alabaster they were when the sun slanted its brightness on them. To us it was a vast playground where, without realising the significance, we found white pieces of bone in the sand which had covered the lost town of Perranzabuloe. In the dunes we tumbled and tossed and shared the joy with so many others during our own years. We took long, sliding steps through the give-way sand to reach the top of a mound where the spiked grass cut our feet and legs. The higher the mound meant a bigger thrill as we leapt into the windy air to land safe and softly many feet below us.

The sea at Perranporth had to be respected. A red flag flew when conditions were unsafe and only summer visitors, those up-country invaders on whom our economy depended, were rash enough to ignore that warning. Hence, when Mother read out items from the *West Briton* in the holiday season, there were always pieces like, 'Drowned whilst on holiday, Mr ... taking a morning dip,' etc. etc. Fury and grief ensued when one of the local inhabitants drowned in rescue attempts. We knew that one must never go into the sea when the tide was going out and it was behind Chapel Rock.

Apart from this, to bathe in the Atlantic was exciting, once again sensuous. The high curl, this I would watch as the chosen wave reached its peak ... and then the anticipation. The fulfilment and the ecstasy as a fierce explosion of white foam crashed against the body! There would be times when I could become as one with the wave, catch it at the moment of turning and ride in front of the swelling foam right up to the flat wet sand.

CHAPEL ROCK — PERRAN PORTH

A Walk by the Fal

Redruth townspeople had their summer gatherings at Porthtowan and from Camborne and Penzance they met at Hayle Towans. Thus, when we stayed at Hayle Towans we met a group of teenagers, just as Cornish but with an aura of dust and machinery around them. The only way I can explain them is, they had a best-clothes-on-Sunday look. Not that they wore their best clothes but perhaps it might be more explicit the other way round. They did not look clean-limbed, brown and stripped in the wind, hair flying and eyes expectant of all the excitement of living. As I consider these words, apart from seeing what a snob I was, I realise that each village or town or hamlet has its own particular atmosphere and character ... even if they are only a few miles apart and each person thinks that his birthplace is superior.

Camborne was a mining town. Nevertheless, whilst on holiday at Hayle, we belonged to a group of teenagers who met daily; sat around, organised games, swam and walked across the Causeway to Hayle itself, past the old Church, to the fish and chip shop. The walk back was slow, ending often in colder air as the end of summer approached.

In the past Hayle itself had been quite a busy seaport, involved with the copper industry and the import of coal. Now the town itself seemed dull and without any character, to us with our own memories. The main street was long and draughty and apart from the fish and chip shop there were no interesting shop windows.

****** ****** ****** ****** ******

He was from Camborne. He was lean with blond hair and had a kind, lazy face. I wondered why he came beside me as I lay, face down on the cropped grass in the hollow where we all met in the afternoons. I was reading a magazine. He said, 'What are you reading?' I turned to show him, then stared at his face which was reaching towards me. I was still, absolutely. He came nearer. His arm was a bar of velvet across my shoulder and I was drawn into my first long, soft and tender and so disturbing kiss.

CHAPTER EIGHT

The Last of the Holidays

Each year there were holidays and places to remember. Holidays which were crowded with young faces and filled to capacity with energy and love. Dear young faces, caught up in the glow of our own ensnaring youth when to stand on a smooth stone, or touch the rough edges of a craggy cliff, to feel the drying of lips on a winter wind or walk on wet sand in the evening when visitors had gone and groups of locals gathered still around their blanket or picnic cloth, was to know the sleek joy of living.

The summer night Uncle Robert stared across from St Mawes to the harbour lights at Falmouth and was so moved by the magic of the sight he was forced to say to his most unimaginative of companions, Uncle Joe, 'Joe ... it's too beautiful ... I think I'm going to cry.'

Uncle Joe snorted. His wry face twisted in scorn and a string of derisory expletives stoned Uncle Robert into silence and stemmed his tears. Joe, whose own facile tears would be roused more easily by more human, down-to-earth incidents with an instant actor's reaction. One who would not waste tears on mere beauty which was to be had for nothing and was all around him.

When we were very young, toddler age perhaps, there are memories, much vaguer, of St Agnes ... Stippy Stappy Lane, and a row between the landlady and Mother about a bath of water in the back yard; myself being chased by sheep ... and of course the raddled red beaches which were slippery underfoot.

Afterwards there were the teenage years of watching boys across the balcony at the Methodist Chapel on Sunday mornings. The years when we developed an interest in fashion and our sunburned bodies were shown off by dresses, not always made by Mother, but sent for, from the papers, Dirndl waists and bright pastel prints, and one exotic summer saw us parade in beach pyjamas, one rose-patterned for Sylvia and one blue for myself.

School was to end in a concentration of mental activity, a frantic revision of all the figures and facts, hammered out or written up on blackboards or marked on text books to be engraved on our minds for ever.

Or at least until the classroom door where we sat our examinations closed behind us and the papers were collected in a box which sealed our fates.

Now we were ready for the world which, even in our far corner of England, was changing its rhythm and shape.

Howard was the first. He was mind deep in the heavy, dull text books, full of worldly financial problems which meant accountancy.

And he wanted to join the navy.

So the end of school did not mean the end of learning. Poor Howard. He became closer to us in those bored years of his. Sometimes he broke out of his studies to stand upon the table as he used to stand, crazily on Black Rock at St Mawes, to preach a sermon, or he would join Sylvia and me in the garden for a few games of badminton.

I discovered that Howard was an asset. I was honoured to become a member of select club made up of Howard and a group of friends. They had names like ships ... HMS *Howey Bay*, etc. I was a Pinnace, a ship that scuttled between larger ships with messages. Like carrying notes to the older girls in school. This was my first introduction to the intricate manoeuvres which were part of young love.

****** ****** ****** ****** ******

Learning to Understand

The hint of a change showed on the beach even though holidaymakers scattered still against the gold strip below the cliffs. This might have been because it was evening and there was this taste of coolness in the air. A coolness that was sharp ... dry wine after the mellowed warmth of sherry. It might have been because there were fewer children now that the main holiday season was past.

Yes, a change of generation.

The preceding weeks had passed under a hot sky. The beaches had been a moving tapestry of tanned limbs, bright cottons, red and blue sunhats, multi-coloured beach balls, green and yellow stripes of deck chairs. Children ran their journeys from the sea to their mounds of sand; carrying their plastic pails of water; patting with energy the timeless shapes of sand castles. Dogs had run with sharp joyous barks of freedom.

And now the scene was slower, shapes were darker; couples moved by the edge of the sea. There was more purpose in their proximity. They were communing, perhaps friends or congenial young marrieds. There was companionship and reason in their relationship.

I thought this and looked towards Father as he breathed in the wet saltness which was carried in the air. The wind came from the rainy quarter and clouds scudded swiftly across the pale sky. I held back my step to match his. Under my feet the turf felt as if it was lifting me, like walking on a firm brush. I arched my feet inside my sandals, revelling in the sensation of lightness. I wanted to spring in the air and run; to feel the wind flapping through my blouse, to make my longish brown hair stream out behind me. I loved this sort of evening. I almost left his side but some new decorum of a near-seventeen-year-old stopped me.

Father said, 'Run ahead, if you want.'

It was as if he had guessed the tension behind my steps.

'It's a pity Joy or Beryl couldn't have come with you.'

These were family friends and I was actually wishing the same. Together we would have soon forgotten any pretentious dignity of young womanhood; forgotten that the end of this summer term might be our beginning and ahead we would have all the licence of adult status.

But ... I would run when I wanted.

'I'm all right,' I said, then realising he was trying to please, 'Perhaps we'll walk quicker.'

Our pace increased as we began to walk on the hard brown path towards the headland. I began to think of a boy I knew and liked, Peter. If Peter were here they would have dawdled. They would have stretched every second so that this walk towards the Atlantic sunset would be deeply pressed inside her. He would have turned to look at me sometimes. I would have seen my ordinary mousy face through his eyes and I would have felt beautiful.

'So Peter couldn't get in.'

He meant the university. I was lucky I thought because I did not have any real plans for my future but I understood enough to be sorry for Peter. He had tried and was ambitious.

'He'll try somewhere else. He did well at school. Bound to get a place somewhere. For a boy a degree is important.' I guessed he was wishing this for Peter so that I might settle. He never interfered but he had said we monopolised each other too much. 'You'll settle down too.'

The tone of voice and his silence spoke of his own achievements ... from nothing. And his children with all their advantages. Suddenly I was on the defensive.

'I think it might rain,' I said.

A watery sun had been blotted out temporarily by a dense patch of cloud. It cleared swiftly. The wind was behind now, sweeping the dappled flanks along.

'We'll go on,' he said. 'Nice bit of air.'

He breathed deeply again. The coolness was clean inside our lungs and he said he remembered the times he had camped here in his army training days. He stared at me. 'I was hardly any older than you are now. Time flies, fast like those clouds.'

I thought of time, turning always, like the spray of the white curved waves below.

'Then there was the war. Not that I want to remember much about that but there was a poem someone from Cornwall had written out there; homesickness was something we all had to find our own cures for ... this poem stuck.' He hesitated a little, then, surprising me,

> 'The West Winds have already
> churned the ashen sea
> and passing it will carry
> the taste of salt beyond the Tamar.'

'Peter will do something, I know.'

I did not expect an answer. Really, this was difficult. If it was possible I would tell my father. But they didn't make any effort to accept a new situation. They had no imagination. Everything was supposed to be as it had been when they were young. Take Father himself, blaming Peter because he couldn't get a place first time. He never went to a university himself; they didn't have to in those days. Of course he had qualified as an accountant, but it was easier then: they didn't have the competition. He was acting as if Peter had failed his eleven plus. We're all lumped together now, I thought, 'teenagers,' not-one-thing-nor-another again. There is no more individuality left. Peter was different. He would make the grade somehow. There we are. We all have to be graded. University years would be wasted for me. Maybe even Peter would find this. Everyone had to be propelled. I thought, I wish someone would propel me somewhere. Into a nice quiet little job like working with books in a library or something.

'Good.' Father brought me back to the present. 'What comes now is the start of something. This poem, he dedicated to his wife, we didn't laugh when he said it. We all felt the same.

> I forget many kisses
> Much love, yet I remember
> Your fire-boned hips, unyielding,
> And the layered granite land.

I mustn't let you think we don't know the answers at our age. Or let you have any ridiculous notion you have discovered love all by yourselves.'

His eyes were looking at the heathered banks, the soft, turfy grass between. Grass that was soft like a thick carpet. A hollow that had been warmed by thousands of suns; that had been sheltered from a thousand storms. 'It isn't only the university. When I was Peter's age I would have given anything to have a chance of a few years freedom ... to look around ... save a bit.'

I said, 'You were different.'

Father smiled sadly. 'We all think we know.'

We were approaching the valley between two sides of the headland. The outlines made a rough frame for the sky and sea beyond. The sky, across which the red streaks flared; the clouds, banded with watery gold. To the west, the yellow, wet sand followed a line of uncompromising cliffs right down to the mists in the distance. 'This won't change either.'

'But they change, they must be different.'

'I was young and felt things more, all that yearning and being homesick and just being married and feeling so ... well, so wanting to live. Not content to be.'

'Well ...'

I saw the break between the two parts of the cliff. Always with Peter, we had to run here; to be the first on the green flat strip between; to see what sort of sky was ours that night. We would look ... for ages. Look right down towards the west. Look at the sea circling whitely at the bottom, sending her spray in little furies or big furies, according to her mood. Then in such a futile gesture to draw it back, over and over again ... endlessly.

I watched the view in front of us and Dad was watching me. I sensed this and we were silent, but there was a difference in our silence. I knew he had been striving to tell me, might tell me still what this had meant. To tell of the times he had made his way, perhaps, to this particular spot; to share with the cathedral cliffs and the roaring plumed sea, the pains and pleasures of his even life.

We both wondered why we had stopped. The breeze was cooler. Suddenly I had to move; move quickly. I looked at him and smiled and caught the warm fondness in his eyes.

'I think I will run on a bit,' I said. 'Maybe over there ... to see the view.'

Father's eyes returned towards the sea in its frame and as I went I heard him sigh.

But I did hear him.

****** ****** ****** ****** ******

No Harbour Lights

Suddenly ... Darkness.

Although it was becoming a bit of a bore it was to be Hayle Towans again this year. A holiday so familiar that the chalet town was a street of friends. Our special gangs changed; there might be a different face and there were changing appreciations.

The river met the sea at right angles and this was dangerous for bathing. Strangers, as they did always in Cornwall, ignored local advice and often an arrogant 'up-the-country' person might have to be rescued from the currents. Frank, who, as I mentioned, was often with us on these holidays, was a strong swimmer. He played for the Falmouth water polo team. Once he and Howard formed a human chain to reach someone who was drowning. Frank waded out with the first of the rescuers, but as Howard said, 'I was the first to lead them back.' There were good stretches of sand dunes and the air in the mornings was clean and salt-washed. We would walk towards the sea before breakfast to sniff the salt air and the morning freshness of the dunes, to enjoy a concentrated smell of bacon and eggs. Plain girls that we remembered from the previous year altered. Suddenly they were not children, there were new curls in their hair and they might be compared to coins fresh from the mint, gold and shiny, jingling with cheap jewelry and attracting looks from the, surprisingly noticeable, males more swaggering than we remembered. Caught in this new atmosphere I became nothing. I thought I had known it all, learnt everything in school, but here I was, legs and arms dark brown, moving across the sand towards the sea and through the sea and through the dunes, just as I was last year. In fact I was worse than last year. I never knew then how small, how unimportant I was. Besides, my nose was pointed. I had a face like a tea-pot, Howard said. My mirror said he was right. The girls around, even Sylvia, had nicer hair, brighter eyes, wore their clothes with much more grace.

And there was a disturbing element in the air. Newspapers stressed the threatening behaviour of the new socialist movement in Germany, the dangerous emphasis on nationalism. We were beginning to read the newspapers with a different intensity. We tried to get between the lines; to size up the strength of a character, the integrity, the willingness or ability of a country to fight. We read a lot about Adolf Hitler and his new Germany which at first had seemed exciting.

Father spoke often about the last war and nothing seemed as if it would go on for ever. It was the first time I looked at something without feeling secure and joyful. Besides, I never liked Hayle Towans all that much. It might have had its history, the Church was interesting and all that, they had imported and exported copper and coal, but it didn't have coves or rocks. It was not as glowingly romantic as St Ives which when seen at night across the water was full of bright trinkets of light and lamps on boats which rocked and bounced in the harbour which was a brilliant arc of scintillating diamonds.

ST. IVES FROM HAYLE TOWANS

The Last of the Holidays

September 1939 ... Our few weeks away were ending. Late August evenings had been stirred by cooler breezes which were exciting but sad. Each evening ended sooner and people remarked as lights came on in the chalets that much earlier to attract the myriad of moths from the dunes, 'Nights are drawing in.'

The wireless was on more often. We were more confident since Chamberlain had been to Berlin and back but there was a dark line being drawn around our lives, ringing happy interludes off all these years as seen on a postcard with a thick edge marking it ... for filing in some vast green cabinet.

The words came over so clearly on the six o'clock news. The announcer (they still prided themselves on BBC English in those days) said each word slowly, weighing its importance before letting it reach across the ether into all those thousands of homes soon to be changed for ever.

We all looked across towards Howard, whose face seemed amazingly set and sweet.

'My playing is over.' That was all he said and we thought thousands of different thoughts.

My Father's eyes were bleak and his face became remote as if he were seeing the battle fields of Ypres once more.

Afterwards we walked to the edge of the dunes to have a last look at St Ives, before the 'Blackout' which had been threatened began.

But there was nothing, just a velvet darkness and a lapping tide on this September evening. The engines in the fishing boats further out in the harbour sounded softer yet more important ... comforting. It was as if they were making the most of the night.

It was the last of the holidays.

The Crystal Moment

Each pebble jewelled the sea bed, with harbour steps
smoothed into stairs; carpeted in green, drowned weed.
The water was melted crystal,
so that to enter was to know the sparkling minute
would be remembered once again
when age would consider sensual yesterdays.

I thought as I lay in the sea's lapping embrace,
even in the callow greenness of my years,
of the time when all this transparency would cloud.

I thought with misted, time-distanced vision,
and for my squandered innocence shed tears.

But the moment passed when the plunging body
split the lighted depths and scattered foam.